HIGHER TEACHING

A Handbook for New Post-secondary Faculty

MIROLAND IMPRINT 29

Guernica Editions Inc. acknowledges the support of the Canada Council for the Arts and the Ontario Arts Council. The Ontario Arts Council is an agency of the Government of Ontario. We acknowledge the financial support of the Government of Canada.

HIGHER TEACHING
A Handbook for New Post-secondary Faculty

John Oughton

MiroLand
p u b l i s h e r s

MIROLAND (GUERNICA)
TORONTO • CHICAGO • BUFFALO • LANCASTER (U.K.)
2021

Connie McParland, series editor
Michael Mirolla, editor
David Moratto, cover and interior designer
Guernica Editions Inc.
287 Templemead Drive, Hamilton, ON L8W 2W4
2250 Military Road, Tonawanda, N.Y. 14150-6000 U.S.A.
www.guernicaeditions.com

Distributors:
Independent Publishers Group (IPG)
600 North Pulaski Road, Chicago IL 60624
University of Toronto Press Distribution,
5201 Dufferin Street, Toronto (ON), Canada M3H 5T8
Gazelle Book Services, White Cross Mills
High Town, Lancaster LA1 4XS U.K.

First edition.
Printed in Canada.

Legal Deposit—First Quarter
Library of Congress Catalog Card Number: 2020947921
Library and Archives Canada Cataloguing in Publication
Title: Higher teaching / John Oughton.
Names: Oughton, John, author.
Description: First edition.
Identifiers: Canadiana 20200368796 | ISBN 9781771835954 (softcover)
Subjects: LCSH: First year teachers. | LCSH: Effective teaching.
Classification: LCC LB2844.1.N4 O94 2021 | DDC 371.102—dc23

To Dr. Francine Jennings,
an inspired teacher of teachers

CONTENTS

■■■■■

INTRODUCTION

■ ■ ■ ■ ■

YOU'RE READING THIS because you are a new teacher, are considering becoming one, or you work with new teachers. You may want to give back to the community, profession or school that helped you, or prepare students to master the job you love. You may be dipping a toe into educational waters with the thought of changing jobs to teaching full-time.

This is the book I needed when I started teaching: a practical primer on the essentials. There are many books about education, but most focus on one or two of the topics that this book addresses. It gives you what you need to start your new job on the right foot. Much of teaching has to be learned by doing, but that's no different than any other profession.

Here you will find only the theory you need to understand current trends in post-secondary teaching. To make this as easy to read as possible, I have minimized direct quotations and citations. However, I would not have improved as a teacher without reading, viewing and discussing others' theories and strategies. When you're ready to explore these issues in more detail, consult the reference list is at the end.

How did **I** become a teacher? Both my parents were the only children in their working-class families to go to university. My father became a zoology professor, my mother a university librarian. Like all my siblings, I completed university degrees. Education and research were in my blood. However, I did not originally see myself as a teacher.

The formal instruction I experienced in public and high school in Guelph, Ontario was uneven. I was not sure I would be good at it myself. When my high school guidance teacher looked at my SAT scores for reading and writing, he said, "You should consider becoming a English teacher." Sorry to say, I laughed, because he was a nice man, and in the long term was right. But at the time, I thought I would become a writer. That's if my career as a racing driver didn't turn out.

My friend and fellow poet Ken Sherman suggested I try teaching at a community college, as he did. "You just do your classes and they leave you alone otherwise. You can write poetry when you're not teaching," he explained. I jumped at the idea, and began my first class not knowing what I was doing. Community college teachers usually have no formal education in teaching, but receive some orientation when they start.

I was pretty terrible, but by observing student reactions, and badgering more experienced professors for tips, I slowly improved. I realized what a privilege this job is. I could support, influence, and sometimes inspire a couple of hundred people every year. Occasionally, my comments made a positive difference in a student's life. I turned one into a reader, and another into a journalism student. There are many sayings about the value of teachers' work, but one I identify with is, "When you cast a stone into a pond, you never know where the ripples end."

I took doctoral courses in education to gain some grounding for my choices and strategies. Then I became a full-time English teacher at Centennial College, a large and very diverse community college in Toronto. When the opportunity came to be seconded into a faculty development position, I applied. Soon I was giving workshops, consulting with other faculty members, and learning about teaching not just English, but everything, so I could be helpful in my new role.

Through talking with teachers in every discipline from fine arts to aircraft maintenance, I began to understand the commonalities and differences in college teaching. I also saw where curriculum originated, what influenced it, and how a badly-designed course could be distinguished from a well-conceived one. As the department grew, becoming the Center for Organizational Learning and Teaching, I continued in my role. I collaborated with other talented and experienced teachers who worked in faculty and curriculum development, led orientation for new full-time and contract teachers for several years, and helped with program review and quality assurance.

My notions of good teaching changed. I realized that presenting new information in a lively and clear way is only half the job. Everyone who knows a field well can talk about it. Teachers must close the loop by finding out what students have retained, and what they can do with it. When the results of teaching are insufficient, one needs better strategies or materials. Teaching is therefore a distinct skill set, which requires close attention to student reactions and work, thinking on your feet, and willingness to try new approaches until something works. It takes patience, perseverance, and the desire to see every student do well, or at least do his or her best. Also, a good teacher is always ready to learn. Each term offers new students; each year brings new technologies, curriculum, and many other demands.

But, as well as being demanding, teaching can be rewarding and even fun. With that in mind, I'd like to share an anonymous limerick that asks an essential question:

> A tooter who tooted a flute
> Once tutored two tooters to toot.
> Now the point that is moot:
> is it harder to toot,
> or to tutor two tooters to toot?

I hope you find this book helpful, and that it helps you along the way to becoming that rare and special person—a good teacher.

1

PRACTICE

CHAPTER 1

WHEN YOU GET YOUR COURSE OUTLINE

■ ■ ■ ■ ■

A COURSE OUTLINE or syllabus has multiple roles. It gives students an overview of what they can expect to learn, how they will be evaluated on their success at doing so, and required texts, materials and safety equipment. For the teacher, it is both a summary and road map of the overall course, giving them clarity about what they should be teaching and evaluating. Also, if it includes a week-by-week plan, it tells teachers when to deliver specific parts of the curriculum and evaluation scheme. It is evidence for the institution that the course meets in-house and provincial/state standards.

When students have successfully completed a course, the outline/syllabus becomes part of the proof used to assess their future requests to be exempted from a course on the grounds that they already have the knowledge and skills listed in it.

In these litigious times, it's important to recognize that the outline is also a kind of contract between the student on one hand, and the institution and teacher on the other. A course outline, particularly one based on learning outcomes, lays out specific knowledge and skills that successful graduates will have. In effect, in return for tuition fees, institutions are certifying that a graduate of a given course/program has attained, to a reasonable degree, all the stated outcomes or objectives. Graduates have sued after they began a job and then were told they would either have to be let go, or at least retrained, because they couldn't

adequately perform one or more of these outcomes that they suppos-
edly had mastered. This happened in Toronto with a student who had
passed a course in business report writing, and was then told by his
new employer that his report writing was well below their standards.
The student won the suit. Such a result points to poor evaluation in the
course(s) in question. It has also, not surprisingly, led to some fudging
in the language of course outlines: "Upon successful completion, students *may* be able to ..."

As for design, sources, and language in course outlines, see the
chapter on "Curriculum."

With all that in mind, now that you've received the outline/syllabus
of a course you've been hired to teach, what to do?

1.   Pay particular attention to the evaluation plan (assignments and
     exams/tests) and required texts and materials, as these are what
     students ask about it in the first class.

2.   Mark each class on your calendar. Watch for public holidays, which
     usually affect Mondays, sometimes Fridays. Indicate when assign-
     ments will be due, and exams or tests will be held. Highlight when
     you need to prepare assignments and tests in order for them to be
     printed or posted before the class. As you develop lesson plans, decide
     when to tell the class of an upcoming evaluation, and include review
     time for it. If you have some flexibility with timing in your course,
     make sure the final assignment deadline allows breathing space
     before exams or other end-of-term assessments. Some e-learning
     platforms facilitate your creating announcements or calendar en-
     tries that appear to students at the right time to alert them.

3.   Ask if your department has an extra copy of the text(s) that can be
     put on reserve in the library for students who cannot afford it/them.

4.   Develop your section outline—a week-by-week summary of what will
     be taught in class, and when each module of the course will be intro-
     duced, covered, and reviewed. In some courses, the week-by-week

may be common to all course sections. Include test and exam dates and assignment deadlines, and then work backwards from these as you develop your lesson plans. Highlight reading, online activities or other homework students need to do, so that you can remind them the week before they're due. Think about when an experiential activity—such as a field trip, simulation or guest speaker—might make sense. Make tentative dates for these and then confirm when you have made the arrangements. Consider, especially if your course is a first-term one for most students, having representatives of your institution's student services—counseling, learning strategists, the library, academic writing center, and peer tutoring—visit an early class to give students a quick overview and identifiable face for their services.

5. Check your section outline against the course outline. Are all learning modules/outcomes addressed somewhere in the week-by-week? Have you included time to introduce, explain, and model the skills for assignments? What about reviewing in the week before exams and tests? Consult the chapters on curriculum and evaluation for help with this.

6. Develop your lesson plans—instructions to yourself on how to make each week a varied and engaging experience for students. Review the chapter on lesson planning to speed this process.

7. Ascertain your department's/institution's expectations for the online elements of the course. Is a pre-loaded course shell available, which you can customize for your classes? If not, is a colleague willing to share with you what he/she has put online for this course? Make sure that, at a minimum, the course outline, week-by-week schedule, and a welcome message including your contact information are posted before the first class. Welcoming students with a video or audio clip is more personal than a document, and gives students a sense of who you are. See the "Teaching Online" chapter for more on this.

CHAPTER 2

THE FIRST CLASS

■ ■ ■ ■ ■

THIS IS THE most important class, because it sets the atmosphere and tone for the rest of them. Will you be friendly, welcoming, and helpful, or stern, remote, and obsessed with covering the curriculum? You will be feeling some stress yourself, but the more you relax (or at least appear to be relaxed), the better it will go.

Students will arrive late, or wander in looking for another class. To help them get oriented, write the course number and title, and your name on the board in big letters.

This is a valuable opportunity to meet your students, learn something about them, and lay the foundation for how you and they will interact. They will be curious about the course, especially what it will require from them in workload, assignments and texts and materials to buy. They may be apprehensive if they have struggled in similar courses in the past. Perhaps other students have told them your course is difficult and requires a lot of work.

It's traditional to devote much of the first class to going over the course outline in detail, but this is not necessarily the best use of the first few hours. It's uncertain how much hard information students will retain from a detailed presentation, as they are coming to grips with a new teacher, fellow students who are strangers, and their feelings about the coming semester.

They are also wondering about you: your credentials and experience in the field, your personality as a teacher, and how you will treat them. If this is your first time teaching, you may not wish to emphasize that fact. Introduce yourself, both as a person, and as a credible authority on the subject you are teaching. Why do you want to teach this course? What will you bring to it? What are your hopes for the semester?

Certainly, present an overview of the required text/materials, overall topics, and assignments. Some teachers put a quiz about the course outline on the learning management system. Students have to pass it before the rest of the content is available to them. Do not ask students who receive an accommodation for a disability to bring you their forms in front of everyone else. Rather, suggest that they leave forms under their self-survey (see below) or give them to you at end of class.

Depending on the subject of the course and the setting in which it is taught, there may be non-negotiable rules around safety equipment and protocols, arriving on time, and so on. Explain these clearly, giving a rationale so students understand their importance. Then put the negotiable aspects of the course on the table. Ask what distracts them during class, and how others can reduce these distractions. It's helpful for students to hear how their behaviour may irritate others in ways that they did not realize. What would everyone like to see in terms of respectful behaviour in the class? How do you want them to address you—as Professor? As Mr. or Ms Surname? Is it acceptable for them to use your first name in class?

Elicit from students a list of ground rules that all will follow in class. As a group, they can volunteer rules for listening to each other, challenging ideas but not their identities, respecting difference, entering and leaving the class in a non-distracting way, and so on. May students eat in class? In a long class, would they prefer to end a little early, or take a break in the middle? If so, how will you know they'll come back on time? Can students use their electronic devices at any time, only when you allow it, or never?

As well as rules, discuss consequences. As any parent knows, a rule without consequences does not last long. When a student is warned about breaking a rule all have agreed on, and continues to act out, you must react. Consequences might include a small fine paid into a penalty jar or box, the proceeds to be donated to a charity at the end of the course. An alternative that does not unfairly target lower-income students is that they have to teach five minutes of the next class. Give them a simple topic—perhaps a review—that they have to organize and lead.

Once ground rules and consequences are agreed, write them down or ask a student volunteer to do this. Keep them available on paper, and on your learning management system so that students who start the course after the first day can read them. This collaborative approach has advantages over your simply imposing a set of rules. One is that people who have had some input into a behavioural code are more likely to respect it. The second is that when a student does cross a line, other students will recall the rules. Rather than a power struggle between you and the resistant student, it becomes the community reminding the outlier of what everyone agreed to.

Students will be less likely to challenge your authority or rebel against the rules if you have a personal relationship with them. The first class is your chance to find out something about them as people and learners. Put together a short questionnaire that asks about their career plans, educational backgrounds, most and least preferred subjects, and learning styles. Sometimes a more generic question such as "What do you like to read?" or "How do you get world news?" can pay off.

Make references and provide tie-ins between lessons/course materials and your students' interests and preferences. They will feel valued and included.

Learn their names as soon as possible. When a student needs reminding of a classroom rule, it is more effective to address him or her by name than by, "Hey, you." In a contemporary diverse classroom, you will be faced with many different names. Make a game of this—ask the student for the correct pronunciation, and get the whole class to repeat it. Memory tricks may help, such as associating their name with where they typically sit, or some aspect of their appearance ("Thomas is Tall"). If students agree, ask to take a picture to insert beside their name in the student list. Another technique is to give students tent cards and ask them to print their first names on them.

Finally, an essential first-day activity is an icebreaker that allows students to meet and get to know their peers. This is especially important in first year, first-term courses, when they may not know anyone else. There are many icebreaker activities listed on the web. One of my favourites is to have students interview each other in pairs or triads and then report the answers to the class. This works well for shyer students, as they do not have to talk about themselves.

Another more entertaining strategy is Body Sort. This requires a room with enough space for students to line up and group in various configurations. Ask them to stand in the room according to where they were born relative to your classroom (the ones born furthest north stand closest to the north wall), or where they live now. Ask them to form groups based on their month of birth, favourite food or music. Invite them to line up according to how many years of formal education they have, how many languages they speak, how many countries they have been to, and so on. They have to negotiate with each other to establish where they belong in the line or room.

One that helps students overcome initial assumptions uses the Venn diagram. Make copies of a blank three-circle Venn. Put students in groups of three, and have them answer questions about their favourite food, music, movie or TV genre, which languages they speak, or where they have travelled. Each student is assigned one of the three circles. When they discover something all three have in common, that goes in the center where all circles overlap. Something common to two but not the third is written where their two circles overlap. Things unique to an individual go only in his or her circle. Ask students to share one thing they all have in common, and one thing that is unique to each.

CHAPTER 3

TEACHING STRATEGIES

■ ■ ■ ■ ■

"Effective teaching is not a set of generic practices, but instead is a set of context-driven decisions about teaching. Effective teachers do not use the same set of practices for every lesson ... Instead, what effective teachers do is constantly reflect about their work, observe whether students are learning or not, and then adjust their practice accordingly."
—**Carl Glickman**

FOR ANY GIVEN topic or skill, there are multiple ways to teach it. Choosing the best approach involves many criteria, including who your students are (their previous knowledge, learning styles and preferences), where the class comes in the course (early or late) and program (first term or final). Is there an upcoming assignment or test that students are anxious about, which some practice would help them feel better about? There are also logistical considerations, such as the classroom or learning space and its furniture (fixed or moveable), the class length, number of students, and available instructional technology.

Before we explore some of the strategies you have to choose from, be aware that teaching strategies are seldom neutral. They embody notions of what curriculum is (see the chapter on this), and even the politics of education. By "politics," I mean some of the issues addressed by Brazilian educator Paulo Freire in his classic work *The Pedagogy of the Oppressed*. Do you believe that the teacher should have all the power in the learning experience, and the student none? Do you agree that the teacher has all the relevant knowledge, students none? Does the suggestion that education should empower students to social and political activism frighten you? If so, read Freire.

There is a useful distinction between three separate models of curriculum and pedagogy. The first and perhaps oldest is transmission. The teacher sends information and skills to the student, who is imagined as an empty vessel filled by the new material. Freire termed this the "banking model": the teacher deposits information into the student's account, and then withdraws it, via a test or assignment, to ascertain how much has been saved. In this model, the student is passive and receptive.

In the transaction model, information is shared and sometimes created through interaction between teacher and student, and student and student. In this model, both teacher and student can act and deliver as well as receive. The teacher knows more about the subject, but also understands that the student may have useful contributions. It echoes the constructivist theory that people actively create their learning, building on what they already know, and adding new layers through discussing, questioning, and testing it with the help of others.

The third model is transformation. Students, and sometimes the teacher, change in an important way as a result of their learning. Education is thus not just the acquisition of new skills and knowledge, but also changes in attitudes, values, and one's world-picture, paradigm or sense of self. A previously reluctant student, one with low self-esteem as a learner, may suddenly find joy and empowerment in learning. A student who believes that refugee immigrants are coddled and overprivileged may, through direct contact with people in that situation, find that his/her notions do not fit the reality of their experiences. For this reason, some learning institutions encourage students to take part in field trips, volunteer work in other countries, or foreign learning experiences. Transformative learning often results.

Let's next look at a common classification of teaching strategies: direct, indirect, interactive, experiential, and individual. As is often the case in education, these can overlap, and a typical class will include at least a few different strategies. You might, for example, use direct instruction to start an activity that is indirect learning, and then have students compare their findings, which is interactive.

Direct relies on the transmission model described earlier. It is teacher-centered, usually featuring a lecture or demonstration, uses closed and didactic questions ("What year did we say the legislation was approved?"), and practice by the "drill and kill" method: do what I say, and keep doing it until you get it right. Direct instruction helps introduce new concepts or skills, and prepares students to undertake an assignment or work in groups in a new way. It is also effective in training for safety and security, where ambiguity or time for reflection would make things worse. For example, if your clothes catch fire, there is one appropriate response: stop, drop and roll. If you are making a left turn into two-way traffic from a one-way street, there is only one correct way to perform it. The weakness of direct instruction for other topics is that it seldom includes a feedback loop to confirm what the student has learned or can apply.

Indirect instruction means that the teacher sets up an activity in which the student learns without being explicitly told what to learn. This can involve inquiry or problem-based learning, when the student, alone or with peers, answers a question or responds to a problem or case study. It is student centered, and puts more emphasis on the process—the how of learning—than on the content. It could also take the form of reflective learning, where students consider something that has happened or they have learned, and write or make an image or video to convey their thoughts about it. Indirect learning embodies some of the principles of constructivist theory and adult education, allowing students to exercise their power to act, question, consider, evaluate and communicate.

Interactive learning is also student-centered. Here the emphasis is on learning with one or more others. It could be using a computer game or program, or online learning resource. It could be one of the classroom apps that let students share and comment, anonymously or not. Often it means working with a peer, in pairs, triads, or small groups. Interactive learning applies the transactional model of education, as learning is created through conversation, questioning, interviewing, and so on. Since most workplaces use teams and groups, good interactive skills are essential for graduates.

Experiential learning is student-centered, but also context-centered. The essence of this approach is that students are immersed in a new role, place or culture, and learn not only the theoretical components, but also how it feels to have one's preconceptions or assumptions challenged. This may align with the transformation model of learning. Typical applications include role plays, co-op or intern placements, simulations, field trips, and experiences in cultures or places new to the students. One key aspect of experiential learning is that, since many of these contexts are unlike simulations or role-plays in not being under the teacher's control, the student's learning and feelings are unpredictable. However, preparing students to succeed in the work place requires some experiential learning, in order to reduce the shock of the real world for them.

Individual learning, as the term suggests, focuses on what a student can learn by him or herself. It is student centered and should be based on what students most need to know, or what they are passionate about learning. It might take the form of a learning contract within a course, whereby a student who is struggling agrees to seek tutoring or outside help and improve this/her classroom behaviour or time management for deadlines. For more confident students, it could be an individualized assignment in which the student chooses the topic or medium. It might be a reading course, the student negotiating with the teacher what material will be covered and how to express understanding and synthesis of it.

Here are some specific ways to use these approaches in your teaching, with a focus on the most common three styles: direct, indirect, and interactive.

Direct

The direct strategy is tempting for teachers because it gives them the illusion they have covered the necessary points for the class, and also because it is often the way they learned themselves. However, telling students what they need to know is only part of the job. If you do so for more than a short time—such as when setting up an activity and giving guidelines, then find ways to make it student-focused. Establish what students have retained and can use. Here are some suggestions:

1. Break a longer presentation up into shorter chunks, about ten minutes apiece. In between, ask and elicit questions; have students quickly discuss the points you made, such as in a Think-Pair-Share activity; do a quick review using a classroom app like Socrative or Kahoot.

2. Give students a structured way to take notes, such as a handout with some blank spaces, and ask them to compare answers.

3. Pose a problem using the information just given and have them solve it in pairs or small groups.

4. If using PowerPoint or other slides, include some questions on your slides. Open a blank slide and type into it student responses. Show them a graphic without a caption and ask them what they think it means or has to do with the directly-delivered material.

5. Tell them you will make a few deliberate mistakes in your presentation about things they should know, and give a small prize or recognition to the first student to spot each one.

6. Instead of just delivering the information, have students create the questions to extract it from you.

7. Break a demonstration into steps. After each step, ask a student volunteer to repeat it while the rest of the class comments.

8. For your learning management system, avoid the easy way to fill in your course shell—a podcast of you delivering a lecture. It is boring video. Find another way to post the information online, such as a series of short videos with links to relevant information after each one, and then an online quiz about it.

Indirect Instruction

Indirect instruction means a facilitated activity. You introduce an exercise, explain why it will be useful and how it will work, give students a time estimate, and then they explore the topic. It can be an individual task, or at first one, followed by a step in which students compare their work or summarize findings to each other. The great advantage of this strategy is, with the right activity, students are involved and engaged. They are probably learning more than they do during a lecture, or at least retaining more of it, because of the task's rich nature and accompanying social interaction.

If you plan indirect instruction using groups, refer to the chapter on "Working with Groups" for a discussion of the issues. Here are some examples of indirect instruction:

1. Reading Circle: As an English teacher, I would often assign a reading and then discuss it in the next class. However, conversations were falling flat. I was supplying the answers. So, I discovered what I should have known. Some had not bought the textbook. Of those who had, some had not read it. Of those who did the reading, some didn't recall much (in other words, they read not to question and retain, but simply to complete homework). I then divided the chapter into two-page sections. Groups of four or five were each assigned a section. Their job was to become the class experts—skim it, explain it to each other, consult their notes, give us key points and ask one good and relevant question. I found this not only improved students' retention of the material, but some of the weaker readers learned from their peers techniques that they had previously shunned like highlighting, making marginal comments, using Post-Its or writing notes.

2. Pass the File: Several file folders each contain a short problem or case study. Students write their solution or approach on the folder, and then pass it on to the next student, who

adds, revises, etc. Continue until three or four students have weighed in on each. To avoid too many students waiting, you could have them do this in pairs or trios.

3. Brief Reflection (One-minute Paper): Ask students to ponder what has just taken place in the class, and then write a few sentences about it anonymously. This can be done on paper or posted via a device-friendly app like Today's Meet. Read out some of these and ask others' views. If time is short, take them with you, reflect, and decide whether the class understands the topic or module, or needs more time with it. It is also an Individual strategy.

4. Gallery Walk or Poster Session: Make posters that display relevant points about the topic. Put them up around the classroom. Students walk around, making notes or answering questions on a hand-out, then return to their desks and share insights. Gallery Walk can also work with components of a machine or system. This is a good re-focusing and energizing activity when students have been sitting a long time, as it gets them moving around and interacting. Split a topic into sections, and assign groups to make a poster for a section.

5. Jigsaw: Divide a topic into suitable chunks, and then assign trios to research their chunk and make a poster about it. Two members then stay beside the poster to teach it and answer questions, while the other one visits another poster. He/she returns, teaches the stay-behinds, and then one of them visits another poster, etc. Repeat until every trio has completed this with the other poster groups. This can be chaotic and time-consuming, but everyone is engaged and it leverages the principle that the best way to retain something is to teach it yourself.

6. The Flipped Classroom: This reverses the traditional approach in which students are introduced to new material in class, and then apply or explore it through homework exercises and assignments. In the flipped classroom, students

access readings, videos and other resources on their own. Class time is used for exercises, applications, discussion, and one-on-one help from the teacher. This strategy can be used with large as well as small classes. One caveat is that it relies on students being motivated and responsible enough to do the pre-homework. Another is that a US study of students in economics and math courses showed that: "the flipped classroom cohort had a 51 per cent larger achievement gap by race, and a 25 per cent bigger gap based on prior attainment" (timeshighereducation.com). If you are intrigued by this approach, try flipping one class, and then see how you and the students feel about the experiment.

Interactive

1. Pause the video: Rather than showing a video straight through and then discussing it, pause it and ask questions, to which students write answers. At the end, ask students to read or share what they wrote. This approach can easily be adapted to a video on a learning management system. There are free and relatively easy-to-use programs which allow you to insert questions or prompts into a video. The video will not continue until the student has responded.

2. Four Corners or Placemat: Get large pieces of square or rectangular paper. With students in groups of four, ask them to write initial ideas or positions on a controversial topic in their corner. They share notes and create a compromise position in the center.

3. As a team-building or problem-solving exercise: give students simple materials and ask them to design and build a structure using only what they are given. One example is to give each group plastic straws, index cards, tape, paper clips, sheets of paper, and ask them to build the tallest free-standing

structure possible. They can then discuss or write about their process. An activity like this is a good way to start a longer group project that will take a few weeks to complete, as it encourages collaboration and bonding.

4. Students design and conduct a survey with just a few questions, either in the class or asking random people in the hall outside. They then summarize their results and give a short presentation saying how valid and representative they think the results are. This aids critical thinking development.

5. Truth Scavenger Hunt: put statements up on the board or screen. Students use their devices to determine which are true or false. Lead a discussion of credible sites/news sources. How can you check a convincing-looking "fact"?

6. Detailed scenarios/case studies for group problem-solving and team-building, such as: LOST LAKE: a general case for problem-solving

Students discuss this problem with their group. In creating a survival strategy, they may use any skills that their group members possess (e.g. first aid, orienteering, mechanical).

Congratulations! You've won a big prize—a fall weekend of fishing and relaxing at a lodge on a remote lake. Included are float plane transportation and accommodation for you and your friends.

Your plane takes off and heads north. Everything goes well for the first hour, but then the motor begins to cough and dies. The pilot, Glenn, radios a distress call, but is too busy trying to glide the plane to determine the exact location. He manages to land the plane at the edge of a small, apparently uninhabited lake, but it crashes into a tree on the shore. The radio and GPS are destroyed and Glenn is unconscious, bleeding from his forehead, but breathing. Quickly, all of you—with cuts and bruises, but no major injuries—get out of the plane. You carefully extract Glenn and lay him on the ground nearby.

Everyone agrees to remove luggage and supplies from the plane quickly in case it catches fire. You find, as well as the clothes and personal belongings everyone has brought, emergency supplies:

> a first aid-kit with various bandages, antiseptic and burn ointment
> a 10-litre jug of drinking water
> six flares
> a tarpaulin
> a box of matches
> two foil "space blankets"
> a fishing line and some hooks and sinkers
> a compass
> a .22 rifle and 20 bullets
> a hatchet
> A box of eight granola bars.

You have smart phones, but cannot get a signal. Night is approaching, and there will be a frost.

Decide, as a group, how you will deal with this situation, and what to do the next day if no rescuers appear. Determine what roles each member of your group will take so that you can survive until you are rescued, or have a found a way to get help.

Experiential

1. Role Plays: write brief scripted statements for three or four students in a role play relevant to a course topic. Ask them to start with the scripted statements and then improvise. They can play parents and teacher or daycare director, customer, service representative and manager. The rest of the students observe and make notes. Variation: if a player gets stuck, can't think of anything, anyone in the audience can tap in and take that player's place, continuing the scene. Make sure to elicit students' feelings as well as thoughts about the experience.

2. Take students into a public area of the building or outside. Ask them to observe things they wouldn't normally monitor, and make notes. For example, do the buildings fit with the landscape or not? What wild animals do they observe? What background noises to they perceive? What is the quietest place? Loudest place? Smelliest place? This exercise can work well for drawing, photography or video classes (focus on something they wouldn't normally); architecture and environmental courses; health and wellness (where do they feel most stressed? Least? Why?).

3. Invite a guest speaker working in the career students are preparing for. But instead of the usual prepared talk, each student has to design one good and interesting question, and then ask it. As a safeguard, to avoid wasting presenter time, audit the questions first and have students revise weak ones. Ask the guest speaker what the best questions were, and why.

4. Disability walk: students go on a brief trip around the building or campus, but some are blindfolded, some have ear protectors or plugs; some need mobility assistance (to avoid having to find wheelchairs, this could just be a rule such as "no stairs" or no distances greater than 50m/150 feet). Each student should have a helper for safety purposes. Ask how differently they experienced the place and what barriers they noted. This suits classes on architecture, engineering, personal service work, etc.

5. The job interview: for a final term, pre-graduation course. Have students dress for an interview, prepare a proper resume, etc. Each student is interviewed for five minutes by a panel of three to four other students while the rest observe. Students can prepare interview questions, as well as the teacher contributing some. Students should not know in advance which questions they will be asked.

Individual

1. Give students an assignment in which they have to choose a topic that interests them. They should write a brief proposal for you to consider before they proceed. You might also give them choices about how they will share the final product—as an infographic poster session, in-class presentation, video, series of songs or poems.

2. Service Learning: students volunteer to help in their communities in some way, and then report on what they learned, what the present service gaps appear to be in that community, what governments or their school might do to help fill those gaps.

3. Co-op/Internship Projects: As well as taking part in a work placement or internship, students in dialogue with you choose a specific aspect they want to focus on, and report on that at the end of their placement. They might discuss, for example, to what extent the workplace reflects the best practices taught in your program, or how the organization/company they worked with is integrating and applying social media.

4. If students (especially those who have so far performed well) argue that a particular assignment does not suit their skills, or is boring for them, challenge them to design one that meets the same outcomes and would take about the same amount of work. Once you have approved it, that is their assignment.

Classroom Variables:

Issues that affect or limit the strategies you choose are the physical size and layout of the classroom, and the number of students in the class. For most learning, the ideal class size is 30-35. The best room is roughly square, with seats and tables that can easily be moved into different configurations, such as a circle or horseshoe; these facilitate open discussion. However, you will not always get the ideal. Problem rooms are long and narrow, so that students are a long way from you and/or the screen, too large or small for the class, and those with fixed furniture.

Class size: Large classes of over 40 make it difficult to use some interactive/experiential approaches. This is especially true in a lecture hall with rows of fixed seats. However, you are not restricted to the lecture-with-questions-at-the-end approach. Techniques that work in this situation include individual work where students grapple with a problem and then share their findings, exercises in pairs or triads; and use of interactive apps or clickers, so that students can see others' answers on the screen.

Questioning:

Whatever teaching approach you choose, how you question students is important in helping build their learning, and to verify what they have understood and retained. Research shows that many teachers ask questions that are not very high in a learning taxonomy. Often they focus on eliciting answers at the knowledge or comprehension levels of Bloom's cognitive taxonomy (see Curriculum chapter). Ask more challenging questions that exercise application, analytical or critical skills. For example, after teaching students a new theory or approach, ask them when it might *not* apply.

Direct them to a brief scenario or case study in their text, or on a handout and ask how well recent course learning can help solve the case. Show them a short video. They make notes and then say what they think was motivating or troubling the characters in the video.

Often, when you ask a challenging question, you will not get an immediate reply. Wait before you intervene with a follow-up, or by answering the question. Most teachers pause only a few seconds, but a good question takes time to ponder. This is learning at its most intensive, as students apply new learning to their previous store of knowledge and skills.

When a question really does not produce an answer, rephrase it.

What do you do when a student responds with an answer that is not what you are looking for? A little reflection reveals that the answer is rarely 100% wrong or irrelevant. This is the time for follow-up questions to establish the student's thoughts. Often you will find that the answer is at least partly on target, but a mistaken assumption or missing step led to the "wrong" aspect of the answer. This is a valuable learning moment for the student and for the rest of the class. Other students more reticent about volunteering probably were thinking along similar lines, and can benefit from your disentangling the right from the incorrect.

REFLECTION

Of the various strategies outlined here, which do you use (or would you use) the most?

Which have you not yet tried?

How can you make largely cognitive material (such as a theory, process or model) into a more experiential and hands-on lesson?

CHAPTER 4

LESSON PLANNING

■ ■ ■ ■ ■

LESSON PLANNING IS both the last stage of curriculum planning and the first of pedagogy planning. Developed in response to a course outline or syllabus with a weekly breakdown of topics to be addressed, the lesson plan specifies how each will be explored and developed during the class. It keeps you on track so you do not omit major outcomes, reminders of homework, upcoming assignments or other deadlines.

If the course you are teaching has been offered for a while in multiple sections, your academic coordinator, Chair, or a more experienced faculty member may supply you with previously-developed lesson plans. If so, it is up to you what to keep or modify. A lesson plan is personal to the teacher. Normally you do not have to share it with others, although you may wish to include a particularly successful one you have taught in your teaching portfolio, with an explanation of why it worked.

Your more experienced colleagues may seem to lack very developed lesson plans, but rather have notes jotted on a napkin or stored in their smartphone. They can get away with this because they have taught the course and know what will work and what won't. What you are seeing is just their reminders, not the whole plan. A new teacher needs a well-thought-out and explicit lesson plan for each class. This makes it easier for you to relax and teach, and ensures that you are helping students meet the outcomes and learn the content for the class. You can work on the less-successful parts of the lesson plan for the next time you teach a given class, while keeping the parts that succeeded.

There are many systems for developing a lesson plan, and I will introduce a few of them. First, what is essential in any effective lesson plan?

Allow a few minutes for community building—letting your students get to know each other and you. This can include a planned mixer or icebreaker, or it can be more informal: a brief open discussion of current events, or the weather, or suggestions for what they would prefer in the classes.

Teachers, especially new ones, are often overwhelmed by the extent of curriculum in a course. They feel that every minute counts, and they must immediately present new information. This is a mistake, because students who are tense or fearful about their progress, or don't feel they have a relationship with you, are less likely to learn. The few minutes invested in a fun activity or a little socializing are not stolen from the serious business of covering curriculum. They are time invested in making students receptive to the rest of the class. It doesn't matter *what* you teach, if they're not ready to learn.

When introducing a new module or theory, find out what students already know or feel about it. You may discover someone has experience or knowledge worth incorporating into the lesson, or you may be able to correct common misconceptions. This addresses both students constructing their own learning, and principles of adult learning.

Second, make connections between the content of this class and both the previous ones (unless this is the first class), and future ones. You are familiar with the curriculum and understand how parts of the course relate, how the skills and knowledge taught in one class are built on, or essential in the next one. But you know the subject better than your students, and have invested time in meta-learning, thinking about how you are learning and making mental bridges. Your students benefit from your making these explicit. Similarly, bridges to their job activities after graduation will increase their motivation to learn. How is a particular theory or model applied in the workplace? What's an example from your own working experience?

A brief bit of jargon: connecting to a previous lesson is called a "backward linkage"; pointing to a coming lesson or assignment is a "forward linkage." A backward linkage is a form of review, and any review helps strengthen those neural networks that retain learning.

Students, especially older ones, appreciate an overview of the lesson. Give them a quick roadmap—a slide, a hand-out which they can annotate, or something written on the board. Be ready to provide a rationale for any part of the lesson, so that when a student asks: "What's the point of this activity or module?", you have an answer that ties it to the course outline and even better, what they will be doing on the job.

As you plan the major part of the lesson that follows these introductory steps, remember the lesson plan is not just about you. The part where you lecture or demonstrate is essential, but so are those where students do something with new information—discuss it, apply it to a problem, connect it to other learning. It is important that you listen and observe how well they master new material, and elicit from them what they are processing well, and what they still need to work on. This is closing the loop, as mentioned in the Introduction. You have to not only put information out, but get it back, and help students make adjustments to improve their understanding and retention. You may have to make changes on the fly as a teacher. When you're lecturing, and student body language and eye contact tell you no one is listening, it's time to switch gears. If it becomes obvious that the way you presented the material or the activities you set up to engage students with it did not work well, use a different strategy.

Think variety. Students have, in general, shorter attention spans and more distractions at hand (those wonderful wireless devices!) than their parents did. Depending on the length of the class, employ a variety of strategies and media. This will help keep students engaged in learning. It also addresses differences in learning styles and preferences. Have one or more activities that get students up and moving, interacting with other members of the class whom they don't usually meet. Think of ways to make cognitive learning happen with a hands-on component—making and viewing posters on the wall, or arranging cards or components in a logical order, and then explaining the choices. Balance between you talking, and the students talking. Include work in pairs, triads or larger groups. As well as typical instructional media like slide shows, demonstrations and videos, try an educational app that students can access with their smartphones or tablets, to have fun with their knowledge and opinions. There are many of these, usually free, including Kahoot, Socrative, Padlet, TodaysMeet, Mentimeter, Quizlet, and Polleverywhere.

As you work on your lesson plan, estimate the timing for each part. These durations should add up to the time allotted for the class, less any breaks. You will get better at guessing durations with experience, but it will never be totally accurate. Depending on many factors, including when the class is scheduled (early morning and late afternoon or evening are problematic for attendance and energy levels), what students have done in the previous class or are anticipating for the one after yours, and the mix of student personalities and abilities, individual classes vary. Your time-management plan may work perfectly for one class, and then another section of the same course takes more or less time with parts of the lesson.

Be flexible, and think on your feet; cut or postpone part of your plan, or extend an activity and spend more time giving students one-on-one feedback. A strategy I suggest for new teachers is to prepare one or two more activities/modules per lesson plan than you expect to use. That way you will not run out of material before time is up. A practical example of giving yourself options for choices in the middle of the class is: if you are using PowerPoint or another slide ware program to present material, include links to external resources like relevant websites or videos. If time allows, open the link and discuss it. If not, advise students to open the link themselves through the learning management system outside the class.

As suggested in the chapter on "Reflective Practice", learn from and with your lesson plans. After a class, write comments on your lesson plan. What went well, and what didn't? When were students most and least engaged? Did a text or video not work well? Keep these perceptions in a file or as comments on the lesson plan. Before you teach this class again, review your notes and make any required changes. Then repeat the process with the new lesson plan.

Models and Methods for Lesson Planning

Robert Gagne suggested that a thorough lesson should include nine instructional events. You can use these as a lesson plan template, filling in how you will accomplish each. They apply equally well to online classes and face-to-face teaching:

1. Gain attention
2. Inform learners of objectives
3. Stimulate recall of prior learning
4. Present the content
5. Provide "learning guidance"
6. Elicit performance (practice)
7. Provide feedback
8. Assess performance.
9. Enhance retention and transfer to the job.

Another common approach to lesson planning has an easily remembered acronym: ROPES. It refers to a five-step process:

R for Review (although some say "Relate"): here you link to students' previous knowledge and learning, either in the course or in previous courses and experiences. What should they already know, or know how to do, in order to master this lesson? Elicit some of this from them; who remembers the theory or model from the previous lesson? This should be brief, about 5-10% of total class time.

O for Overview—a quick look at what is coming, including a rationale based on the course outline or the workplace, and perhaps a teaser for something that you think students will enjoy, such as a chance to employ their beloved devices, a competition with a prize, or a funny video. Around 5–10% of class time.

P for Presentation: here you present, or facilitate the students' interacting with, the new material. This may be a lecture or mini-lecture, a video, slide show, demonstration, or group discussion on parts of the material (e.g. each group masters and summarizes pages of a textbook). This should be about 30% of the time.

E for Exercise: Students engage with the new material, try it out, discuss it, and apply it to a case study, problem, or puzzle. Here the most important learning takes place, so allot about 40% of class time. Remember that it should include E for Evaluation by you: observe how and what the students are doing and give them informal feedback. What are they doing well? What are they missing? How might they do the task differently or more efficiently?

S for Summary: what are the main things learned or practiced? It is usually more effective, when time allows, to extract this from the students rather than do it yourself. Making them think about their learning and sort out key points is important both for their overall understanding, and for increasing retention by accessing those new neural networks. The remaining 10% of class time should belong to this stage. You can relate this step to the next class or an upcoming assignment, providing a forward linkage and helping them anticipate it.

Finally, some instructors prefer the similar but six-step BOPPPS planning approach.

The acronym represents an effective lesson plan's parts:

Bridge-in, Connect this lesson with previous ones, perhaps add an icebreaker.

Outcomes (**o**bjectives), similar to Overview in ROPES.

Pre-assessment. This is the added step, establishing what students already know or feel about the topic.

Participatory learning. The Exercise stage.

Post-assessment, Check in with students to establish how much they have mastered.

Summary, and link to the next lesson or upcoming homework, etc.

Queen's University offers a handy BOPPPS Infographic and some suggested activities at http://www.queensu.ca/teachingandlearning/modules/active/18_boppps_model_for_lesson_planning.html.

CHAPTER 5

TEACHING ONLINE

■ ■ ■ ■ ■

MOST INSTITUTIONS OF higher education now have a learning management system (LMS). This is a web-based platform for course-related materials, activities, and communication. The earliest, WebCT and Blackboard, are still in use at many places. Competitors include Brightspace (formerly Desire2Learn), Moodle, Canvas, and others. All do roughly the same things, although their features and ease of use vary considerably. They allow access to course documents (outlines, schedules, faculty contact information, assignments, readings and links). They support media such as PowerPoint and various video and audio formats. They may include email and chat room options, and facilitate students doing group projects on-line. Some offer utilities like a grade book, which automatically calculates marks. Others allow faculty to view reports and statistics showing which students have logged in and for how long.

Some offer, or are linked to, a virtual classroom like Adobe Connect —a platform for online conferencing and webinars. These offer video and audio channels for the teacher/presenter, a chat pod, file-sharing space, and a whiteboard which can show drawings, slides, documents, or share the teacher's desktop to show an outside resource, video or site. These support an online class in which the teacher can be seen and heard, and students can ask questions and respond to them. There may be useful add-ons like a tool for surveying student opinions and sharing the results.

Such a session can be archived for students to watch later. If you expect to use live video of yourself frequently, invest in a decent webcam and headset with microphone, so sound and video quality is good. Most laptops and other devices today have built-in webcams and microphones, which are useful when the other equipment fails (it will!) or for brief appearances.

The degree to which faculty use these resources varies considerably. Many teachers, especially those accustomed to face-to-face classrooms, use the LMS as an archive, posting a few documents and PowerPoints or podcasts of their lectures. Students are not expected to interact much with such materials, and generally don't. Some institutions expect teachers to not only post course outlines, contact information and assignments, but also use the grade book so that students track their own progress, and the final grade is sent to the student records system.

Other faculty make an effort to include videos, quizzes, and some live sessions. They may teach a class online, a great option when the school is closed due to weather or another problem, or if the teacher has to travel but still wants to deliver a class. Some teachers offer a student contact hour online, using email or the chat function to answer students' queries.

There are a few different formats for classes that use an LMS. They can be traditional face-to-face (F2F) sessions, with the LMS as a backup for a few resources and course documents. They can be blended, also termed hybrid, by having part of each class online, or whole classes online along with some F2F sessions. Finally, they can be completely online, with no F2F sessions.

Many institutions demand more classes on line simply because they are cheaper to deliver— they don't need classroom space, markers, or photocopying. Faculty can teach from home, therefore not requiring office space. There is also an advantage for students who would rather learn at home. Online classes can be synchronous (live) or asynchronous, meaning the student can learn and participate at any time. Asynchronous online learning suits students with jobs or childcare issues, because it allows them to access learning whenever. Surveys show that students say online learning, when well designed, is as helpful as F2F.

However, if someone asks you to take an existing F2F course and put it online, know that it takes considerable effort and ease with the technology to create good online learning experiences. Simply dumping slide shows, podcasts and documents in there won't work. Not all academic managers recognize that more time and work are needed to create a good online course or class than an F2F one. The many things you might say in a regular class have to be written, or recorded as video or audio, and then uploaded and tested. Also, not all teachers are good at everything. They may have little design sense, struggle with software, or post writing with grammatical and spelling mistakes. For this reason, institutions are increasingly hiring instructional design specialists who help faculty with online technology and suggest the best ways to deliver specific modules.

As in the F2F classroom, teacher presence is important. Post a friendly letter or video introducing yourself and outlining the course on the first page or module. Throughout the course, students should be able to see your picture, and hear your voice, live or recorded. Lessons should have an easy-to-find introduction or overview, a rationale for the activities, a variety of strategies and media, and a chance to review what's learned. Students should be able to apply what they've learned and get informal feedback from you before they are graded on it. Keep students from getting bored by varying how you present material. Make some of it interactive—quizzes, scavenger hunts, games, videos interrupted by questions or response prompts—so they do something other than look at the screen.

In a typical virtual classroom, you have a choice of standard layouts, such as conferencing, collaboration, and presenting. Each uses different sets and sizes of "pods" (individual modules such as whiteboard, chat, file-sharing, and live video). Learn how to make these full-screen, rather than always staying in the predetermined layout. For example, when greeting the class or introducing a topic, make your video full screen. Do the same for slide shows or videos; then return to multi-pod layout. Most allow you to stream more than one live video or audio feed at once. This can become chaotic, but it does allow you either to share the screen with a student—who is answering a question in detail, or giving a mini-presentation—or turn over control of it (as presenter) to another colleague or a student.

Remember, too, that you may have classroom management issues online. Sometimes the relative anonymity of online spaces emboldens people to say things they would not utter in person. Post guidelines for respectful communication online. You can, with some systems, vet each asynchronous comment by students before it appears to others. With more mature students, you might skip this step. But when a student comment does cross the line, you must react quickly, removing the comment and informing the author why.

Students should not struggle to find the learning materials and activities for each module. When we developed the learning management system pages for our "Teaching and Learning in Higher Education" program at my college, each course had a similar on-line look and structure. Lessons had a menu with all the weeks/modules listed, and each week had a "Start Here" file which alerted students to what was expected, and provided links to activities and materials. If an academic program persuades all its teachers to adopt a consistent on-line course approach, it makes things much easier for students. They do not have to figure out the LMS approach for each class, but simply follow the pattern they are used to.

Remember that students associate computers and screens with entertainment and choice. They skim and click until they find what they want. Design your LMS materials accordingly so they have some options, and there are occasional entertaining bits, like short, funny videos or games.

Try to make your introductions amusing and engaging. If it sounds boring, students will be less likely to explore what you want them to learn. They resist reading long documents online, or watching an hour-long recorded lecture. (Would you enjoy it?) Also, keep accessibility in mind. How will you meet the needs of deaf or visually impaired students in your online materials? What design techniques can help? Your center for students with disabilities can probably help with recommendations and examples. Have a forum or discussion page for general issues (such as materials/links not working on the LMS, or suggestions for better materials) as well as for specific topics connected with a module.

Remember the principle of active learning. Rather than simply having students watch a video or slide show, insert questions or prompts for discussion (free online programs such as Educanon help you do this). Then review their responses, or post them for all to discuss. Ask students to find and post links to resources that they find helpful.

When you have the materials and activities uploaded, switch to "student view". Try each link, document and video. When one doesn't work, note the problem, until you have gone through everything. Then fix the problems. You can now share the pages with reasonable assurance that most students will be able to use them.

Of course, the downside of any technology is technical problems. If you decide to teach in a virtual classroom, students at home will have issues that they need help with by phone or email. They may have Internet access problems, an unusual or outmoded operating system, or an incompatible browser. Before you teach a full virtual class, do a practice session with students to sort out these problems, and make sure you know how to use the options to switch from the virtual classroom's desktop or pods to a full-screen view, or to go to an external site or video and then return everyone to the classroom, and to put students into separate discussion groups and return them to the whole class.

Having hosted a number of webinars, I recommend you make a checklist of steps and follow it religiously. Test your microphone and webcam, and have back-ups ready. The time you don't verify your microphone, headset or webcam's functionality is the time it will fail, while everyone's watching. In my experience, sound problems are most common, and often the hardest to sort out. If you neglect to record or save an online session, it's gone forever.

Online learning in its various forms is here to stay. Like classroom teaching, it can be done well or badly. A good way to learn what works is to take an online course yourself, and tune into live or recorded we-binars. Ask colleagues who appear to be skilled at working with the LMS what they would advise; even better, ask if they will give you access to one of their courses to experience it yourself. Note what you find as best practices, and then try to replicate them when you are designing your own online content and activities.

REFLECTION

What on-line resources do you learn best from? Can you model any of these in creating on-line media for your course?

Are you at ease when being recorded or "broadcasting" via a video camera and microphone? If not, how can you get some experience and feel more confident?

CHAPTER 6

CLASSROOM MANAGEMENT

■ ■ ■ ■ ■

ONE OF THE less pleasant tasks for a teacher is managing the students so that the class environment is respectful, safe, and considerate. Even though most of your students are legally adults, they may not always behave that way. You should be prepared for disruptions and interpersonal conflicts—with you, and between students themselves.

Issues that arise and require classroom management strategies are intertwined with other aspects of teaching. If you get to know your students as individuals, use a range of teaching strategies and materials, are willing to listen to and implement sensible suggestions from them, and keep your patience and sense of humour, you are far less likely to face major classroom management problems.

What position will you take on the classroom management style spectrum? At one end is the authoritarian, who has little interest in students or their preferences, and is very task-oriented. The authoritarian's motto is "My way or the highway." At the other end are the laissez-faire teachers who set few boundaries and easily get off track, wasting time. Their classic phrase is: "Whatever you want." Both types face student behavioural problems that are partly their own fault. The authoritarian inspires rebellious and individualist students to push back. The laissez-faire teacher will face challenges both from motivated students uncomfortable with a chaotic classroom, and from others who attempt to take it over.

By following the suggestions made in this chapter and others such as Instructional Materials, Teacher Presence, Evaluation, Assessment and Evaluation, and Teaching Strategies, you will find a place somewhere in the middle of the spectrum that will reduce behavioural issues, and help keep the class on track and engaged with the lessons.

Once you are a few weeks into the course, solicit feedback from students on how it is going for them. This should be anonymous, and should not take too long for students to complete. In my experience, surveys done in the classroom get a higher rate of response than online ones. Their results are a great source of advice about how to modify your teaching style or materials. They also act as a safety valve, for students to alert you to anything troubling them. If you do not seek such feedback, you run the risk of the classroom environment deteriorating as unhappy students stop coming or act out in class, because you have not addressed something they dislike.

If it is an issue you cannot change, such as the assigned text or evaluation plan, at least acknowledge you have heard their concerns, and find some aspects of the course which can be modified to make them feel happier. A quick and easy classroom assessment tool is Stop, Start, Continue: students list one thing you are doing as a teacher they want you to stop, one thing you are not doing you should start, and one thing that is working well and should continue. In the One-minute Paper, they write a quick response to a prompt like "What the worst thing about this course?" This technique can be used to debrief at the end of a module, and check on how well students have mastered the content and skills taught. This is also true of Think, Pair, Share, in which students are invited to reflect for a minute, discuss their thoughts with a partner, and then share them either with you (via notes) or the whole class, if they are willing. Device-friendly apps that do not reveal users' names, like Mentimeter, Padlet or TodaysMeet, are useful to get quick feedback that everyone can see.

If a student confronts you or is otherwise being disruptive, stay, or at least appear, calm. Reacting angrily only escalates things, and tells the student how to push your buttons. Remind him/her of the ground rules and state how the behaviour has to change. If the student continues to be disruptive, ask him/her to leave and to meet you later.

In this case, it is helpful to have a third person join in to provide an objective view and alternative strategies. Your academic manager, a counselor, or dispute resolution specialist can help. You may ask that the student sign a behavioural contract, indicating how he/she will change, and the consequences for failing to do so. Keep a written record, including dates and times, of each significant disruption. Unless the student behaviour stems from a personality conflict with you, it is quite likely to be repeated in other classes. Documentation can help your academic manager or security officer decide how to handle the situation.

Boundary Issues

Your job is to foster students' learning and evaluate their progress fairly. However, some students will attempt to cross your professional boundaries. If you hear comments like those below, draw the line politely but firmly, and when appropriate, refer the perpetrator to a counselor or other person who helps students deal with non-academic issues.

"Teacher, you're so hot!" This is probably addressed more often to women teachers than men, but we've all heard sad stories of teachers who get involved romantically, or sexually, and then pay the price for it—public condemnation and loss of their job. There's a simple rule to follow: keep students at arms' length until they have received their final grades. Then you cannot be accused of favouritism or scapegoating, in the case of an affair gone wrong. It's not surprising that students sometimes develop crushes on their professors. They look at you a few hours a week, sometimes daydreaming and fantasizing, and your position carries respect and authority. But your job is to be mature and remind them that you are there to teach them, not be their friend or date prospect. If they persist, send abusive or inappropriate messages, or try to meet you outside the institution, let Security and, when necessary, the police know about it.

"I couldn't get this assignment done because of [my life problems]."

Deal with assignment issues by granting an extension or alternative assessment, if it is merited and allowed by the course guidelines in the outline. Students you develop some rapport with—especially those who feel isolated, or unsupported at home—may divulge problems with relationships, finances, visa status, abuse, and addiction. Listen, if you have time, but caution them that you cannot help with these issues; that is a counsellor's job. Refer them to the appropriate person or office, and walk them there if they are in crisis.

"Can I share a secret if you promise not to pass it on to anyone?" The correct answer is "no." The role of teaching does not guarantee confidentiality about what students tell you. In fact, if a student communicates indications of suicide, violence towards others, or abuse, you must share this. Tell your academic manager, Counselling or Security. Don't ignore signs of trouble and then have something terrible happen because no help was offered.

"I really need to get my grades up in this course. Can we work something out?" Unless that something is alternative or extra work allowed by course and institutional policies, and the student completes it, say no. Students may try bribes, appeals to your compassion or threats to improve their grades. Resist them. The grade must be based on their work as evaluated by you according to course standards. If you made a mistake in calculating grades or forgot to include a completed assignment, of course you should fix it.

"You're so helpful! I wish you were my parent." Sadly, this may be true, but you didn't sign up—nor are you paid—to foster a lost child. As before, express your sympathy, but refer them to a counsellor.

"I emailed you at three in the morning and you didn't reply right way!" Explain in the first class that you are not available 24/7, but will check your voice mail and email every day, so messages will receive a response by the next weekday. Don't give out your personal phone number; student calls should go to your office extension.

Here are some specific classroom management problem personalities, and strategies for dealing with them.

The Dominator: a student who is more aggressive or experienced than the others always volunteers answers to general questions, talking over others without letting them finish. One response is to direct questions to individuals, especially those who tend not to volunteer. Another strategy is to give each student three tokens or cards. Each time they answer, they forfeit one, until they have no more turns. If a student continues to dominate the discussion, meet him/her outside class and explain why the behaviour is a problem.

The Sidebars: Students who frequently hold off-topic discussions, either audible ones or using their devices, impede not just their own learning. They distract you and others. Raise this issue in the class ground rules discussion and get a consensus. If students need repeated reminders, either institute a no-devices policy, or move them so they do not sit together.

Students Who Attack Individual or Group Identities: When a student makes a statement—racist, sexist, homophobic, or otherwise objectionable—that targets a whole group or an individual, react immediately. Explain that that is hurtful, and if there is time, discuss why. If not, meet the student outside class. Do not let the comment slide. Other students want you to intervene. If you don't, you give tacit permission for future such comments, and they no longer feel safe in the classroom.

Public Enemies: Sometimes students bring conflicts that have nothing to do with your subject or classroom management style. Perhaps two of them had an argument or fight in the past. They may represent groups in conflict in another part of the world. A practical fix is to have them sit away from each other, and not to put them in the same group too often. However, this is also a teachable moment. In the workplace, they cannot refuse to work with others, regardless of identity, or serve only certain customers. Mention this, and offer some peacemaking/listening strategies. Also, remind them of ground rules for respectful discussion and confronting ideas and factual claims rather than an-other's identity, religion, or politics.

Late Arrivers/Early Leavers: In the ground rules discussion, agree on ways for students to enter or leave without causing disruption. Designate seats closest to the door as "reserved" for students who arrive late, or must leave early. If students habitually come late or depart early, find out why. It may be that they have daycare, transportation, or job issues. Express compassion, but also explore ways that they can attend more of the classes. If students are late for an early-morning class simply because they won't get up early, one strategy is to hold pop quizzes worth a few per cent at the beginning of the class.

The Challenger: a student who questions your ability, identity or credentials to teach the course, or who vocally expresses dissatisfaction with teaching strategies and materials, should be invited to a meeting. Some students will oppose teachers who are female and/or appear young. Explain why you have the knowledge and experience to teach the class in a firm, non-defensive manner. Where the issue is assigned texts, videos or the like, solicit their suggestions for alternative strategies or materials. You may be able to turn an opponent into an ally.

The Class Clown: They love to tell jokes and get the class laughing. If you don't control these students, they will turn many classes into a back-and-forth between your instructions and content, and their one-liners and asides. The best strategy is a one-on-one meeting. Explain that, even though you find some of the material funny, it is distracting for others. Offer the chance to do a joke of the day at the beginning or end of class, and give other students similar "spotlights," so the focus is not just on the clown. You might ask a student who takes excellent notes to do a summary at the end of a class or module, or invite one with design experience to put together a slide or poster for the next class. A variation of the Class Clown is the Re-director, who may not have a punch line ready, but often tries to insert a discussion of some other issue in the news that is troubling them. As with the Joker, don't let them hijack your class and lesson plan. Try leveraging class consensus with a little humour: "I'm sure you'd get lots of responses on your favourite social media platform, but we're all here to day to talk about _____ and help get you ready for your next assignment. Do the rest of you agree?"

Me, Me, Me: A student who is struggling with homework, or unhappy about an assignment or test grade may monopolize class time to argue the issues with you. Remind the student that class time is for everyone, and your office hours or before/after class are for individual issues. Similarly, the student who arrives late and then demands a recap of everything previously covered should access notes on the learning management system, from you after the class, or from a friend.

The Silent Partner: A student who never participates in classroom discussion or group activities may just need encouragement. There might be larger problems around social anxiety and alienation. Using icebreakers and assigning group members randomly, rather than letting students always choose their partners, may help. Students who are self-conscious about their accent or spoken English skills may be more willing to add their voices in an online forum, or by using a classroom app such as Socrative, TodaysMeet, Padlet or Polleverywhere.

The Interested Outsider: Students whose parent, spouse or partner is very concerned about their academic progress may ask you to speak to or email that person. Do not do so. It is up to the student what to tell people in their families or relationships. Explain that right-to-privacy legislation prevents you from discussing student's work and grades with others outside the institution.

CHAPTER 7

TEACHER PRESENCE

■ ■ ■ ■ ■

TEACHING IS A performance. Before you say anything, students are watching to determine the kind of instructor you will be. Will you be friendly, good-humoured, stern, task-oriented, relaxed or helpful? Your appearance and body language start to answer these questions, and once you speak, more boxes will be ticked in students' mind. First impressions are important. It's harder to change a mistaken one than to begin with a blank slate.

You will succeed at fostering information and skills if you can easily get students' attention, entertain them, and speak effectively. One way to become more effective is to improve your presentation skills.

If you can't be heard clearly by some of the students, if you talk too quickly to be followed by non-native English speakers, if you mumble or mispronounce words, or your delivery is so monotone that listeners fall asleep, not all students will absorb what you are saying. Another common mistake is lack of eye contact. Teachers often multi-task, speaking while doing something else—writing on the board, pointing to a slide, or manipulating equipment. However, if your eyes don't meet students', they soon lose interest in your words. We know how quickly people can be distracted by their own priorities or a device.

As with any skill, practice makes perfect. There are tried and true ways to improve public speaking: Toastmasters Club and taking part in debates are useful. So is watching someone who is good at working a room: an experienced teacher, a politician, a comedian or a motivational speaker. Instead of focusing on the content, watch how they engage the whole audience and individual members; how they move around the room, use gestures and eye contact; how they vary voice tone, pitch and volume; when they pause, check in with the audience, or adopt a new strategy. Then develop those skills yourself.

Some of your best allies in improving these skills are non-human: a mirror, a video camera, and a digital sound recorder. If you can get a friend to watch you and comment, even better. An observer will note things you might ignore.

Practice the skills and techniques listed below, and monitor yourself trying them. What works best for you? What adds some drama or interest? Do you have any distracting mannerisms or physical tics— playing with your hair, stroking your chin, fidgeting, adjusting your clothing? Often we are unaware of these until we see ourselves as the audience sees us.

Stance and Posture

Find a way to stand in front of an audience that is both secure and relaxed. A stiff, ramrod posture implies that you are stressed or an authoritarian; leaning on furniture or a wall suggests you don't really care enough to command the space. Try standing normally, feet about shoulder width apart, and keep your weight evenly distributed over both feet. This reduces the risk that you will indulge in distracting side-to-side or front-and-back swaying.

Now think about your vocal projection system. Sound starts in your larynx, makes a 90-degree turn, and exits from your mouth. You want to keep your throat and jaw as relaxed as possible, and your chin up to speak effectively. Also, aim your speaker system—your mouth—at the audience as much as possible. Don't talk to the whiteboard, the ceiling, or the floor. This not only makes it harder for you to be heard, it also reduces eye contact. If you look at your audience, you will speak to them.

Gestures are an important part of your communication tool kit.

They are so instinctual that people use hands and body language during a phone conversation. Keep your hands free. Don't bury them in your pockets, clasp them behind your back, or distract yourself and the class by toying with a pen, marker or other unneeded prop. It's fine to rest your hands on a podium or table while talking, but don't put any weight on them.

Also, practice moving around the room. Effective speakers don't stand stock still for long. Nor do they endlessly pace back and forth, distracting listeners. They move when there is a reason. For example, if part of the class or audience seems uninvolved or distracted, walking closer invites them to refocus and pay attention. If a student asks an interesting question, you might approach him/her, which also gives you a few seconds to consider your response.

Spending long in one corner of a room is a bad idea, because it reduces your interaction with those sitting furthest away. If the room or classroom has an electronic podium in a corner, use a remote control or mouse so that you can occupy the center and move to the opposite side. If you are speaking while using the projection screen, the best place to stand is at one side of it. There you can maintain eye contact and quickly check what's on the screen without turning your back. For variety, go to the back once in a while, so you are facing the same way as the onlookers. This tactic also helps the students in the back focus.

Voice

Consider your voice. You may not especially like the sound of your speaking voice, but remember that you hear it differently than others do, as it reaches your ears through vibrating your bones and soft tissues. This is partly why your voice will sound different when you play back a recording. The good news is that, however your speaking sounds now, you can improve it.

A couple of tricks will help before you teach. Relaxing your whole body, especially your throat and jaw, is one. Spend a few minutes tensing and then releasing muscles. You can do this sitting at a desk, so it doesn't have to be a public performance. Make sure you are hydrated, and take water to the class with you. Dry vocal cords are unhappy.

Many vocal performers—singers, announcers, public speakers—do some form of vocal warm-up before they're on stage. Humming can loosen your muscles. So can singing, if you have a place where you can get away with it. Tongue twisters are a good workout, especially if you mispronounce words and names, or stumble over phrases. Try some of the classics like "She sells seashells by the seashore," and "How much wood could a woodchuck chuck?" I am fond of "Inexplicably mimicking his hiccupping, she amicably invited him in" and "Rugged rubber baby buggy bumpers." Say these several times over, gradually increasing speed.

Consider your voice's tone variety. If it is monotone, find ways to relax your throat and jaw muscles. Tight muscles don't provide much variety in tone. Try saying things with various tones—surprised, ironic, questioning, serious, dramatic. Use these to vary your delivery in class. Make sure that when you say, "I'm happy to meet you all and teach this course," you sound like you mean it.

As well as tone or timbre, you can vary the pitch of your voice—both how high or low you speak, and as a way of stressing certain words. Inexperienced speakers tend to drop pitch at the end of a sentence or phrase; you hear this with business owners who voice their own amateur commercials. Keep pitch level at the end of a statement, or raise it to convey excitement. There is a distinction between the way trained announcers do this, and the pitch rise that signals a question. Listen carefully until you can reproduce the difference. However, raising pitch at the end of every sentence sounds like you are questioning your own words.

Good volume and projection make sure that your audience hears you. In a medium to large classroom, without a microphone, you need to speak loudly enough that someone with less-than-perfect hearing sitting at the back or side can hear you clearly. This means, depending on room size, background noise, and acoustics, you will need a volume approximately twice that of a normal conversation with someone standing near you. Check this by having a friend or colleague sit at the back and tell you what is loud enough. Memorize that setting, and then add another click-of-the-amplifier-knob of volume when the room is full of students. Of course, it never hurts to ask the class at the beginning if everyone can hear you. Once you have students' attention, vary the loudness, sometimes dropping it as a form of emphasis. Watch their body language and facial expression. When you are getting signals that they can't hear you, crank it up again.

Projection is the art of throwing your voice to the back of the room. Stage actors learn to do this; remember the difference between a normal whisper and a "stage whisper"? Much of projection, as mentioned above, has to do with facing your audience, keeping your chin level or raised, and maintaining eye contact.

What about verbal tics? Most of us add fillers when our minds are in neutral but our mouths are motoring along: *umm, ahh, er, like, so, eh, again, well, you know?* and their many cousins. A few will not cause major problems, but many are distracting. The audience gets preoccupied with the next time you'll insert a tic into a sentence, losing track of your subject. These tics are a symptom of nervousness or not having planned the presentation well, so you are at a loss where to go. You can reduce them by giving yourself good notes to speak from, and rehearsing on your own what you are going to say.

Finally, there is the issue of speed. In an informal situation, such as talking to a friend or colleague whose English skills match our own, we happily speak about 250 words a minute. Excited speakers—or those doing commercials and trying to get all the fine print into a few seconds —almost double that speed. For teaching, especially when the material is new or difficult, or if you have many non-native English speakers in the class, speak more slowly. Pause after every few sentences and check how the class is responding. If people look puzzled, try to rephrase, give a different example, or ask them what they understand.

When I began teaching, I often spoke too fast. Students would note this on feedback forms. I adopted strategies like pausing after every three or four sentences, and putting Post-It notes on the podium reading SLOW DOWN to remind myself. I may still vociferate too quickly at times, but I've learned to note the signs and respond accordingly.

CHAPTER 8

INSTRUCTIONAL MEDIA

■ ■ ■ ■ ■

COMPARED TO A few decades ago, when instructional media consisted of the blackboard, mimeographed hand-outs, an overhead projector, and the odd 16mm film or VHS video, choices are much wider. I will summarize some of the drawbacks and advantages of in-class technology and learning management systems.

A few classrooms still have traditional blackboards with chalk, but they are rapidly becoming outmoded. Perhaps this is a pity. Just a century and a half ago, Josiah Bumstead wrote: "The inventor of [this] system deserves to be ranked among the best contributors to learning and science, if not the greatest benefactors of mankind."

Computer and Digital Projector

Now built into most classrooms, these facilitate projecting slides, photographs and other graphics, spreadsheets, documents, webpages and videos. However, "death by PowerPoint" is the approach of many teachers, who revert to the role of lecturers accompanied by overcrowded slides. This is an uninvolving and very teacher-centered way to instruct. Teachers should approach the free slides offered by textbook publishers with caution. Many of these are simply bullet-point lists that students find boring. Relying heavily on them tells students that you are not invested in creating good and personalized audio-visual aids to support their learning.

Slides are visual. They should show pictures, maps, simple charts, and graphics with as few words as possible. If you want to give students a lot of text, use the textbook, a handout or your learning management system where they can read it at their own speed. The two most common complaints students have about teachers' slides are: 1) many words on every slide, often in small fonts; and 2) reading every word out loud. Since students read faster than you can speak, don't read slides out; speak to them, questioning, expanding, and indicating alternative approaches. Make your slide shows interactive. Pause and ask questions, or insert a mysterious image and ask what it means. Have a fill-in-the-blank question occasionally. Leave a blank slide and type in student responses, thus giving them credit for insight and adding a variety of perspectives.

For the images you use on slideshows (and the LMS), you are free to use clip art/stock photos that come with programs like PowerPoint, and your own photographs or drawings. You cannot download the majority of images from the Web without incurring copyright problems. However, if you search for "creative commons" images, you will find good pictures that the creators have given varying degrees of permission to use. If you need images of a special industry or technology, ask your administrators if they have bought CDs or web licences for such collections. These are fair game, because your department paid usage fees by buying the collection.

There may be copyright issues with videos unless they are from your institution's library, or your department has bought the rights. You usually can show videos from social media sharing services like YouTube and Vimeo, if the work was posted by its creator. However, if someone shares a clip from a copyrighted production such as a feature movie, TV show or news broadcast, you would be infringing copyright by showing it without first getting written permission from the rights owner. Your institution's library may be able to help you with questions concerning fair usage.

Keep in mind that many stock images and videos may not be representative of the diversity in your class. If your students are only shown images of young or middle-aged Caucasian models and actors, where do they see themselves? Often, with a little research, or by asking colleagues or your library, you find media that portray more diversity.

Remember the sacred mantra ABB—Always Bring Backup. If you usually store shows or data on a USB drive, add a copy on your email or a file-sharing site where you can access it if the USB drive fails or you lose it. Keep a paper version with you in case the projector and/or computer malfunction. That way you can still talk, employing the original teaching medium. If you experience a technical problem: 1) ask students to help, as they're often more knowledgeable than teachers; and 2) don't spend more than five minutes solving it. If the issue persists, give up and move on to another mode of delivery. Respect student time.

There are many potentially useful videos available. How-to and instructional shows are posted on video-sharing sites such as YouTube and Vimeo. Choose wisely, however. The ideal video should be short (ten minutes maximum), engaging, recently made, technically good, and of obvious relevance to your topic. Give your students a work sheet to fill out during the video, or assign them questions to discuss after viewing. Don't be afraid to pause the video and ask questions that will help their thinking, or push them to address questions raised. For critical incidents or scenes packed with significance, rewind and replay. If students express dissatisfaction with a given video, ask them to find a better one. Recognize their effort if they do so.

Two common technical problems come up with videos. One is sound: there are often three or four separate volume controls when showing a video in class, and all of these must be up for decent volume. As well as the volume icon on the computer desktop, there may be a control on the video player app, and on the podium or room A-V control panel. It's best to test a video before students are in the room to ensure nothing is on "mute" and the sound is adequate. The second common problem is videos not starting or freezing due to inadequate Wi-Fi speed. If this occurs, ask a technically adept colleague to help you download future videos so you are playing them from a file, rather than over the Internet.

A lesser-known piece of classroom technology that can be useful is the document camera. Essentially a video camera on a stand, this has zoom and focus controls that allow you to capture a small object or a document or graphic and project it on the screen. It can be useful in writing classes, when you want everyone to look at a written sample or student's draft. It can also be helpful in technical classes to highlight details of a map, schematic, diagram, or small component. Document cameras are sometimes built into a drawer that pulls out of the podium, so are not even noticed by some teachers.

The whiteboard remains a good teaching tool. If you want to demonstrate calculations, logical problems, circuit designs, or sentence choices, it's a quick way to share and then modify something. It requires fresh erasable markers, an eraser or cloth, and some modest drawing ability, or at least the skill of printing clearly. Also, while you are working on the board, you lose eye contact with students. More than a few minutes of this, and their attention drifts. For detailed designs or sequences, prepare them ahead of time on a slide or handout.

Our students use their devices to research, store information, and communicate (see further discussion in the "Learning" chapter). Rather than banning them outright, it's more helpful to consider when they can be used to assist learning. With the growth of wireless devices, many software designers have created free and useful classroom applications or apps. These allow you to design an activity in which students use their devices for an educational purpose. You might poll them for their opinions on an issue, ask for their opening thoughts, or have them try review questions. Students can compete in groups to answer a game-show-like series of questions, and see their scores and ranking after each question. Usually, you create a free teacher's account and design the activity ahead of the class, which takes a few minutes. However, apps require enough student devices, and sufficient Wi-Fi speed and capacity to handle the data.

CHAPTER 9

MANAGING GROUPS

■ ■ ■ ■ ■

HAVING STUDENTS STUDY and work in groups is important for multiple reasons. It develops career skills, because organizations and companies assign employees to groups for task forces, hiring committees, quality circles, and teams. Group activities develop soft or generic skills employers want: interpersonal communication, effective listening, negotiation and compromise, time management, delegation, persuasion, and summarizing. Also, groups prepare students for the reality of workplaces in which they collaborate with people of different ages, ethnicities, religions, and experiences.

The more socially skilled enjoy group work. Others will tell you it is a waste of time, and they work best on their own. You might accept that argument if your students are going to be self-employed, but even the lonely writer or artist in a garret has to pitch ideas and meet with editors, storyboard artists, publishers, and clients. So the best response is "Thanks for telling me that. Now is your chance to learn some ways to make group work less painful for you."

What can you assign groups to do? Some common approaches are Buzz Groups, quick discussions for two to three minutes, to brainstorm or get reactions to a module you have just taught; problem-solving or team-building exercises involving building or designing something;, and developing strategies based on a scenario. Another common task is to get them to review reading/videos assigned for the week, or previous in-class material, ask them to highlight the three or four most important points/ideas, and create one good question about them. Traditional exercises like scavenger hunts around the building or online for facts and images, debates on a controversial topic and role-playing are also productive.

The most frequent complaint from students who have completed a group project is that grades do not reflect the varying levels of effort within the group. A way around this is covered in the "Evaluating Groups" section of this chapter.

Preparing the Ground

While Western educators and their students take group work for granted, this is not the case with all cultures. Students whose previous courses were more teacher-centred often feel that the professor should lecture, while they take notes for the exam and test. When put into groups, these students may think: "The teacher has all the knowledge! We don't know anything. Why is Professor making us waste time like this when we could be learning?"

You may have to spend a little time, therefore, giving your rationale for group activities and assignments. But it is essential, when you have students who either shun groups or have little experience of them, to give them tools and strategies so that they can succeed at working with others.

One resource that may help is a model for understanding group processes, Bruce Tuckman's Forming, Storming, Norming, Performing (1965). He suggested that groups go through steps in order to complete a task. Forming includes initial introductions, discussion of the task, and suggestions about how to proceed. Storming is when conflict rears its head, and arguments ensue about whether one person should lead or all take equal responsibility, the best strategies, and the nature of the task. Students need to learn that this is normal group evolution, and can lead to an effective process that everyone can live with. Storming is only negative when a group gets stuck and becomes dysfunctional because it can't resolve internal conflicts. Some suggestions for active listening strategies, conflict resolution, and techniques for compromise (like the Four Corners exercise in the chapter Teaching Strategies) can help here.

By the Norming stage, there is agreement on a workable process and the role for each member. Having a note-taker will help solidify these guidelines. Here groups develop basic project management skills, agreeing on a timeline for tasks and the sub-steps necessary to accomplish each.

Performing is the creation, tweaking and submission of the completed work, as a presentation, written report, or media project. Some now add a fifth stage, Adjourning, which involves the project's wrap-up and debriefing of the participants.

Group Roles

As well as a little group process theory, students benefit from a clear idea of the different roles they can take in a functioning group. When you put students into a group for a brief discussion whose results will be shared with the class, you might appoint, or let students elect, a:

- facilitator to keep the discussion on track and involve all participants;
- timekeeper who helps the facilitator guide the group to task completion in the time allotted;
- recorder, who notes the key points raised;
- and reporter, who shares these with the whole class and adds his/her own insights. With groups of four, everyone can have a role.

You might share examples of helpful and ineffective group behaviours. Build a list on the board by asking for suggestions: for example, those who can provide a coherent summary of a discussion, or help resolve conflict between others. When faced by an example in their own group, students can then say "Stop being an X... let's get back to the task." My list would include the Joker, the Re-Director, the Grumbler, the Always-right Arguer, the Sleeper, the Distractor ("Oh look, a squirrel!"), Ms Excuse Me, I Only Talk to My Friend Here! and Mr. Count-Me-Out.

A colleague of mine who often taught classes with many non-native English speakers gave them handouts with sample phrases helpful in group process, and ones that wouldn't be. Instead of "That's a stupid idea", one might suggest "Interesting. Can you tell me more about how that would work?"

Assigning Work and Forming Groups

It is essential to provide clear instructions to groups, whether for a brief in-class discussion or for a more extended project. Give the rationale for making this a group activity. Set a deadline or duration, and let them know whether this is flexible. How long a presentation, report, or other product do you expect? Making sure your instructions are explicit will save the groups time, as they don't have to figure out what they're supposed to do, just how to do it. Write steps and outcomes on the board, and give reminders as the deadline approaches.

For most purposes, four or five students per group is optimal. Too many members, and the group becomes hard to manage, often dissolving into non-productive subgroups. Too few, and there is not enough variety in skills and perspectives to get the job done well.

Should you allow students to choose their own partners, or assign them randomly? There are arguments for both strategies, and you will decide based on your knowledge of students. If, for example, you have several students who struggle with spoken English but are fluent in another language, it may benefit them to work together early in the course, developing their group skills and not worrying so much about their accents. However, letting students work in another language comes with a condition; at least one of them must be able to translate for you how they are doing, and summarize the results in English for the rest of the class. Another issue with letting students pick their groups is you may have a few students—culturally distinct, or shyer—whom no one picks. You don't want to abet the perception that the class consists of groups of friends, and one of "losers".

Assigning members randomly to groups models the workplace better, and develops student skills in communicating with differing others. It pushes students to perform more effectively. When a friend might let someone goof off, another student may remind the slacker of the responsibilities and ask for more effort. This is especially common if you have a mix of ages and experiences in each group. Older students generally have more pressure on their time and less patience for wandering off task, and they will go parental on the off-task individuals, helping get the work done.

Another option is to form groups based on what the members have in common, even if they don't already know each other. For example, you might give them a learning style questionnaire and form groups according to predominant style, or go by birth month or season.

In-Class Groups

Once you have set the groups up and given them their tasks, let them work. But observe them, and intervene if they seem to be off-task, or have reached an impasse. Watch for groups where the majority participate, but one or two seem alienated or uninvolved. One strategy to integrate these students is to ask them for a summary of what the group has done so far, and then ask the other students if they have anything to add. This can help drive home the message that listening in a group is as important a skill as talking.

It may be tempting to dissolve a dysfunctional group, but they will not learn important conflict resolution skills if you do. Instead, discern the problem, and ask group members individually for a strategy to overcome it. You could have them write these down anonymously, then draw and discuss them until the group has agreed to a specific strategy. You can suggest one, but it's more effective coming from them.

It can also be useful to make quick notes about each group as you observe them. Are all members present? Is everyone participating? These can be useful back-up for your decision-making if, later on, group members complain about the performance or attendance of a member, and argue that he/she should not receive the same grade as the rest of them.

When groups are ready to debrief, find ways to give each group equal time. If all groups were working on the same task, don't ask one group to tell you everything they discussed. Some of the points will be similar to the remaining groups'. If you only ask the other groups if they have anything to add, you are not validating the effort they put into developing all their points. They will wonder about the worth of the whole exercise. Instead, ask each group for one point, and keep going from group to group until all ideas are discussed.

Long Group Projects

If you assign a major project during which students work in the same group, create checkpoints so you can make sure they are roughly on schedule and task. For something that takes a month, have one check-in each week. These do not have to be full meetings with you and the group. You can visit the groups if they are meeting during class hours, or have them email you.

If a group seems seriously dysfunctional, try the strategy mentioned above to draw solutions from the group itself. If they still are stuck, you may be faced with reassigning them to existing groups. Don't do this late in the project, or they will not feel accepted by the new group, and it may be difficult to gauge what each has contributed to the final product.

Evaluating Group Work

Design a clear rubric (see next chapter) or set of criteria, and share these with the students when you introduce the assignment. Make sure there are marks awarded not just for the final product, but for the process. This also allows you to negate the almost-inevitable complaints like, "I did nearly all the work, and Siraj did nothing. Why is he getting the same grade as me?"

One way to do this well is to design the evaluation instrument so there are marks for the quality of the product—presentation, report, media creation, etc.—and for the group process, how effectively members communicated with each other, and the attendance, participation and effort of each member (see the Evaluation chapter for a sample rubric). This latter part should be filled out and marked by each student, so they grade their own contribution as well as their peers'. You have your notes on their in-class work and attendance in case they try to award their friends unrealistically high marks for little work, or conversely, collude to scapegoat a group member who did the work but is not liked by the others.

Most students, in my experience, are honest about grading their own effort, sometimes more critical than the teacher would be. If you think the grades given by students are out of line, ask for copies of their contribution (e g. drafts, slides, etc.).

CHAPTER 10

ASSESSMENT AND EVALUATION

■ ■ ■ ■ ■

MEANINGFUL EVALUATION OFTEN stresses teachers and students alike.

So much for students is predicated on getting the right grade: scholarships and bursaries, promotion from one term to another, graduation, getting into a graduate program, or winning a job after graduation. Students are pressured to achieve high grades not only for these reasons, but also to meet both their own and their families' expectations. For international visa students, academic results influence their ability to stay in the country.

This pressure on getting the right grade makes students anxious before major tests and assignments. It leads to depression, even suicidal thoughts, when they get a poor result. It also contributes to conflicts between student and teacher over your calculations, fairness, and the instructions given.

Grading is the *least-favourite* activity of most teachers, but the *most important* role of teachers according to many students. Part of the reason for this is how educational institutions have made grades so crucial. Students are responding to the social and cultural emphasis on grades as the proof of being well-educated and accomplished. Many students now think that paying tuition means they should get the grades they want, since they are "clients" of the institution.

This stress on the exact grade sometimes obscures the most important aspect of evaluation: its role in teaching and learning. You, as teacher, can learn from grades. Grades inform you how well individual students and the whole class are doing, and also how you are teaching. They can alert you to flaws in the evaluation scheme, or specific assignments and test questions. If, for example, a class of generally hard-working and competent students performs more poorly than expected on an evaluation, is it their fault, or yours? Is there a lack of clarity in instructions or questions, or not enough scaffolding for students to meet the challenge?

Grades should play a similar role for students. A fairly-arrived-at-grade gives learners a sense of how well they are doing in the course, what specific knowledge, skills and attitudes they are struggling with, whether they need to work harder or differently, and whether they are likely to pass. Keep your accompanying comments as clear as possible, and review how you arrive at grades on an ongoing basis. It helps them make decisions about dropping a course before the academic penalty deadline to reduce their course load, or whether they should alter their homework and time-management plans.

With the value of evaluation as a tool for teaching and learning foremost in mind, let's look at some of the varieties and aspects of evaluation.

Types of Evaluation

Diagnostic: determines a student's strengths and challenges in specific skills (such as a writing sample) at the start of a course or program. Usually has no grade attached.

Formative: students can learn from the grade and feedback, and make appropriate changes in future work in the course. Thus, feedback in evaluations has to be specific.

Summative: Indicates overall level of accomplishment at end of course or module. There is no chance for the student to learn from this, other than to work harder in future courses.

Capstone: a complex assignment, often a simulation, which requires students to apply previously-learned skills and knowledge.

Evaluation Feedback Guidelines

Don't highlight every error in student work with a red pen. Instead, identify common problems, and give an example of each in the students' work. Explain where they can get help to redress these problems. This saves you work, and is less depressing for them. Remember when your own assignments came back covered in teacher's ink? Even if some praise was included, it never made up for all those highlighted mistakes.

Try the sandwich approach. Say something positive (the first slice of bread), include the meat of where they could have done better, and follow up with another slice that recognizes what they did well.

Evaluation design is influenced by the curriculum approach, and should match it as much as possible. Often the curriculum approach is mandated by a government directive. For those new to outcomes-based curriculum, learning outcomes are:

- measurable, observable performances
- within an industry-specific context.

Here's an example: "Upon successful completion of this course, a student will write a well-structured news article."

Consider the difference between measuring **knowledge** and measuring **a performance** of it. There is further discussion of this in the Curriculum chapter.

Also, keep the five characteristics of effective feedback in mind when responding to student efforts:

Focus—Discuss the task/process, not the student
Comparison—compare the students' work to course outcomes or their previous work, not other students'

Achievement—give praise for what was done well and explain why

Improvement—specific suggestions for how the student's approach and performance could improve

Tone—feedback should be constructive, motivating, encouraging.

Alignment

Ideally, in effective outcomes-based curriculum, course outcomes are aligned to program outcomes and generic or soft skills outcomes; evaluations are aligned to course outcomes. "Aligned" means that each evaluation relates to one or more of these outcomes, and is an effective way to measure them. By the end of the course, all outcomes should have been assessed by one or more evaluations.

A valid evaluation in an outcomes-based system, therefore, should observe and measure a performance of an outcome. Suppose that the outcome to measure is "Communicate effectively with others in pairs or small groups." How would you assess student progress on this so there is no mismatch between outcome and evaluation approach? Early in the process, a test or assignment on which they define and apply basic terms and concepts of interpersonal communication makes sense. But, before the course or module is completed, the student must be observed communicating with others, and graded on that performance. This is the only way to be sure that the outcome is assessed.

Grading Approaches

Holistic: an overall impression of accomplishment/quality. This is appropriate in cases where the student performance is an artistic or creative project where overall effect is most important. However, since a holistic judgment is subjective, the grade may be hard to justify.

Checklist: indicates which steps in a procedure or process were completed. This is effective for evaluating procedures in which performance of each step is essential. The grade is simply a total of the number of "correctly performed" steps. A checklist is also helpful for students when you hand out an assignment that has multiple steps. Students can note that they have completed each part.

By criteria: establish key aspects of performance, and evaluate the quality of each to arrive at total grade. This works for most types of outcomes and goals, and both teacher and student can quickly recognize the aspects that are well performed and those that still need development. A rubric is the easiest way to record and represent evaluation of each criterion.

An effective rubric has three to five criteria, usually in the left column, and three to four levels of attainment, usually in the top row. It captures important elements of the performance in the chosen criteria. It has descriptors in each box, such as a summary of what a level 2, or basic, performance of criterion 1, would look like. It is shared along with the assignment so students can see how they'll be assessed. This reduces questions from students about what you expect in an evaluation. Although rubrics are very helpful in providing transparent evaluation to students about where they are succeeding or need to do more work, they may inflate grades. It becomes easy to evaluate specifics but not the whole, particularly on more creative projects.. You may want to add a separate component for a quality judgment.

Here's how to design a rubric. First, analyze the assignment you are giving. Settle on about four to five aspects, or elements of the performance, that are the most important. These are your criteria. In a presentation, it might be: structure and content of presentation; use of voice; body language; audio-visual/media use; audience involvement. If there are minor things to evaluate, you could have a criterion called "Other" with a list of what these encompass. Now decide how many levels of accomplishment you want to grade. Those who design surveys with Likert (numbered rating) scales suggest that an even number of choices is better, because those who fill the scale out may be tempted to just check the middle position (e.g. 3 on a scale of 5) rather than think hard about whether the performance was worse or better than average. Now, design a table. I used word processing to do this, but if you are comfortable with a spreadsheet program, create the rubric as a spreadsheet with a formula that automatically totals the grade. It should have a column for each of your grading levels, plus two more, and enough rows for your criteria, plus a title row. It will look like this.

Criteria	Poor	Fair	Competent	Exceptional	Row Total
Criterion 1	Descriptor 1	Descriptor 2	Descriptor 3	Descriptor 4	
Criterion 2	Descriptor 1, etc.				
Criterion 3					
Criterion 4, etc.					

TOTAL:

Now fill in a brief descriptor for each of accomplishment of a criterion. With a presentation, for example, if Criterion 1 is "Use of Voice", the Poor/level 1 descriptor, earning one mark, might say "Volume too low, monotone, frequent verbal tics." Level 2 might represent two of these mistakes, but the third aspect is done well. Students who read these understand what exactly you are looking for in a good presentation. If you want to have more affirmative quality categories, use terms like "Beginning," "Adequate", "Accomplished" and "Excellent." Once you have designed a good rubric, grading student work becomes faster and more objective. It also tells you what **not** to grade. For example, suppose you are evaluating an assignment that has frequent grammar or spelling errors. If you didn't make this a criterion, you can comment on it but not deduct marks for it. Use the rubric when teaching students the skills you want to see in the final product or project.

Exams and Written Tests

Tests are best for recall/comprehension of material, and simple applications such as a short case study, solving a calculation, or other limited problems. Well-constructed exam/test questions can measure some higher-level thinking skills through asking students to identify cause and effect, or rate solutions in order of effectiveness, with a rationale for their choice. Written answers allow you to evaluate both quality of thinking and quality of expression. Many students are stressed by upcoming tests and exams. If your institution has learning strategists, ask one to visit and offer some tips on effective strategies for answering test and exam questions.

Multiple-Choice Question Design

For assessing basic course information, a multiple-choice test question has a stem (set-up), a correct answer and plausible distractors (incorrect answers). Each answer should follow the stem in grammar, and be of similar length. Some students know that teachers tend to make the correct answer the longest, since it is the one they care about. Check that no questions are ambiguous, and that each question has only one correct answer. Have a colleague complete the test. This will reveal any confusing or poorly written questions. It's possible that your textbook publisher or department can supply good test questions which you can adapt.

Alternatives to Exams and Written Tests

Project/simulation: requires observation and effective rubric/evaluating scheme

Performance of outcome (e.g. presentation, maintenance procedure, role play, mock interview)

Portfolio containing a range of artefacts/evidences of performance (includes documents, assignments, pictures, journals, plans, etc.)

To make students less resistant to, and worried about, evaluation, allow them some choice in the process. You might give students the option to do an online presentation (video, narrated slide show, animation) instead of a traditional in-class speech with slides. To ensure students show each other attention and respect during presentations and demonstrations, include a grade that reflects their comments on/evaluation of other students' work.

Group Work Assignments

NAME	Attendance / 5	Effort / 5	Leadership / 5	Cooperation / 5	Attitude / 5
Self					
Member A, etc.					

You can alleviate the most common evaluation problem in group work: students complaining that one or two did all of the work, yet other members who contributed little receive the same grade for the assignment (see The Managing Groups chapter).

Here's an example of a student-evaluated rubric; a separate rubric would be filled out by the teacher to evaluate the overall product or project. Also, the teacher should discuss with students how to evaluate the more subjective categories on their rubrics, giving examples.

PARTICIPATION RUBRIC FOR GROUP WORK

Student Name: _____

Project Title: _____

Add a row for each additional member.

Teacher calculations: each student's participation mark is added from these rubrics, then divided by the number of members to determine the average participation grade.

Now, add this participation grade (out of 30) to the project quality grade out of 70. The result is the student's overall grade.

Reflection

As a learner, what are your favourite and least favourite ways of being evaluated?

Why?

Does being evaluated make you feel stressed? If so, how do you control your emotions?

How can you get students to focus on what they are learning and retaining, not just the grades they receive?

CHAPTER 11

ACADEMIC INTEGRITY

■ ■ ■ ■ ■

AS SOON AS someone invents a test, someone else invents a way to cheat. Cheating and plagiarism continue to be common in higher education. Dealing with them is time-consuming and, depending on your institution's policies, may require several forms and meetings. As with classroom management, these problems compel teachers to act as enforcers, so some let all but the most obvious cases pass without comment. While tempting, this behaviour can lower an institution's graduation standards and reputation.

Teachers and future employers want students to work hard and earn the grades they receive. Students who commit academic integrity infractions are evading learning. They are cheating not only themselves, but also future employers and clients, who expect someone with their credentials to know all the important aspects of their job. Why do students who cheat their way through a degree or certificate program end up devaluing the institution's credibility? At some point, they will reveal ignorance of something they should know, leaving the observer to question why they graduated. When I discussed academic integrity with students, I would ask: "Would you want your airline pilot or heart surgeon to cheat on tests and exams? How about your lawyer?"

Academic integrity problems do not exist in a social vacuum. For one thing, higher education's emphasis on written examinations, tests, and quizzes pushes students who are lazy or underprepared to cheat on them. Instructors who repeat exactly the same tests, exams and assignment year after year tacitly invite students to give copies to friends and siblings who follow them a term or year later. Courses that have very heavy workloads may make students feel the only way to pass is to cheat. Also, we live in a culture which tolerates much dishonesty, even rewarding it. How many politicians caught lying or breaking laws go on to be elected? How many guilty celebrities have been let off criminal charges or given light sentences because they are famous?

In addition, our ideas about intellectual property and authorship are changing thanks to the prevalence of digital devices that instantly copy and transmit texts, images, music and movies. If journalists and academics copy and paste others' work into their own without acknowledgement, and consumers illegally download and share music and movies, why shouldn't students apply the same methods to their work?

However, there is good news: attention paid to how you teach, and how you design tests and evaluations, can minimize the occurrence of such problems, saving you time and grief. Let's look separately at the two horns of the academic integrity demon: cheating first, then plagiarism.

Cheating

Cheating on tests and exams can be done many ways, but most often involves a couple of approaches; the traditional one is the individual student accessing "cheat sheets", prepared notes that he/she brings in on paper or a device. Notes can be hidden in hats or inside clothing, or sometimes the nearest washroom, if bathroom breaks are allowed, or written on the body. For entertainment, search for "test cheating" on YouTube, and you will find many helpful short videos that show ways to hide notes inside pens, on the backs of rulers, even under Band-Aids. If you prefer anecdotes, consider this: a professor at a Toronto-area college grew suspicious during an exam when he noticed a student studying his water bottle. It turned out the student had scanned the label into a file, replaced the fine print with exam notes, printed a new label, and affixed it to the bottle! You can find instructional videos for this method as well.

To minimize such attempts, look at your test and exam questions. If they are too far down Bloom's cognitive taxonomy, relying only on recall and comprehension of formulas, definitions, and facts, they invite this type of cheating. However, if you ask questions that involve students' personal experience, and require critical thinking, analysis, or synthesis, they cannot rely on cheat sheets. Similarly, open-book examinations are quite difficult to cheat on. The information is there, but the questions require students to use different parts of the text and exercise their minds. Some teachers encourage students to prepare one page of notes that they can use during the exam; this reduces the impetus to cheat, and in deciding what to include, students are thinking critically about the course contents in a way that benefits retention.

Technology can also facilitate cheating. This is true not just in the obvious ways: such as a student accessing notes on a smartphone or smart watch, or photographing a test and then sharing the image with classes who will have the same test later, or students using devices to communicate during a test. If you set online quizzes or tests, a student can log in and then have a friend answer the questions. Some new testing programs incorporate a video feature that allows professors to see if a student gets up during a test to be replaced by someone else, or to access the Internet on a second device.

If you use multiple-choice tests answered on cards processed by a Scantron or similar machine, be aware that some generations of the machines can be flummoxed by students using lip balm to run a waxy strip down the card's left side. Machines vulnerable to this technique will mark the answer card 100% correct regardless of the actual boxes filled in. Reliance on evaluations more sophisticated than multiple-choice questions will reduce this type of cheating, as will spot-checking unusually correct cards to see if the answers match the answer key.

Another good strategy is preparing three different tests for each class, drawing on a bank of good questions at a consistent level of difficulty. This way, students on either side of an individual will have different patterns of right and wrong answers. One professor told me that simply printing the test on different colours of paper led students to assume that the tests were different. They spent less time trying to copy each other's answers. Also, as suggested above, do not repeat exactly the same test or exam term after term. Vary them to reduce the risk of students inheriting last year's version.

You can reduce the pressure on students to cheat by addressing their anxiety about mastery of the material and what will be on the test. The week before a major test or exam, review relevant material by having students answer, or even better, create good questions, and then discuss which answers are the best and why. If your institution has learning strategists, ask one to visit your class and talk about legitimate ways to do better on tests, such as answering easy questions first, skimming all the questions to budget time, and allowing a few minutes at the end to review and, if necessary, change answers.

The second major type of cheating is collusion. Students work out a strategy ahead of time for signalling each other by patterns of coughing or pencil tapping to ask for answers in multiple-choice questions. They may pass notes, or sit so that someone can easily see and copy their answers. Interestingly, research indicates that male students are more apt to cheat on their own; female students are more likely to aid someone else by collusion. A simple way to reduce such problems is to assign students seating during a test or exam according to their last names or student numbers, or entirely at random. It's much harder to collude from opposite sides of the room.

When supervising a test or examination—called invigilating in Canada and proctoring in the USA—make sure you do an effective job. Do not use the time to catch up on grading or class preparation, so that the students are not being supervised. Instead, move around the room from time to time. Pay special attention to the back row, since this is where cheaters will congregate. Standing behind students will ensure they behave, since they can't see where you are looking.

Plagiarism

This is the act of copying someone else's work and using it without credit. The problem occurs in many spheres. Journalists, authors, scientists, songwriters and others have faced lawsuits and other consequences when caught plagiarizing.

When considering an act of plagiarism, it is important to talk to the student about it. Cheating is almost always intentional, but students may genuinely not be aware that writing or copying images from others has to be accompanied by citations or references. They may feel that information is communal. They may also come from an educational culture that values collective creations above individual effort.

Suppose you are assigning an essay, research paper or project in which students may be tempted to use plagiarized material. Make the students aware of both the institution's policies and your own expectations. Show them examples of both correctly referenced and plagiarized work. Also, model how to create a proper reference in the style you prefer. Have them do a sample quotation as a reference from a textbook and show it to you for feedback. In some institutions, librarians or academic writing center tutors will visit classes and give workshops on these issues.

There are many sites and services called 'paper mills' that offer pre-written papers to students. Some will create custom assignments. A good way to reduce such issues with plagiarism is to break major assignments into steps. If you require, and award marks for, preliminary versions such as a proposal, outline, and rough draft, students who would submit a paper written by someone else will have to work backwards from it. First they must get you to approve the proposal, and then write a rough draft with realistic mistakes, which is more work than simply following the rules.

Avoid assigning topics too general or common in the discipline. Make them more specific by requiring use of the student's own experience or community, or a current news story as a case study. Another good strategy, especially for fast-changing fields like networking, social media marketing, and biotechnology, is to require that all references be from sources less than two years old. Many paper mills sell essays and reports written years ago. A good example of this involved a professor who thought a paper sounded familiar, and then realized that she had written it herself as an undergraduate. When her former professor retired, he put years of graded assignments out in the hall for recycling. Someone scooped them up and scanned them into a paper mill's database.

If your institution subscribes to a plagiarism-checking service such as Turnitin, much of the detective work will be done for you. If not, you may have to copy suspicious chunks of the paper in question, and search for matches on the Internet. However, these approaches can be beaten by students trading papers that are not available on the Internet or in the database of a plagiarism-checking service. One way to reduce problems is to ask students for a low-stress writing sample early in the course. Get them to write a couple of paragraphs about their career plans or a similar innocuous topic. Tell them this is a writing diagnostic or get-to-know-you exercise, but keep a copy of each student's paper. You now have a portrait of their command of grammar, punctuation, spelling and vocabulary. When you are looking at a suspect paper, compare it with the sample. A quantum leap in style, structure, or vocabulary means you're looking at another writer's work.

Also, plagiarists who are lazy or rushed often give away the game. You might notice, for example, that the introduction and conclusion are written in a notably less confident and correct style than the body of the paper. You may find apparently random font and formatting changes caused by incompetent cutting and pasting. Perhaps the references are all from obscure or long out-of-print sources. You might even spot the source URL helpfully printed along the bottom of each page.

A good way to verify your suspicions is to meet the student, and then ask whether he/she understands the paper, can define difficult words used in it, or explain the thesis and how it is developed.

If it becomes evident, based on the meeting and your own research, that a student has plagiarized, follow your institution's academic integrity policies and procedures. If these allow faculty discretion, however, first ascertain why the student plagiarized. Was it deliberate, or inadvertent—a result of not understanding the rules? If so, this is a good learning opportunity. You might allow the student to redo the assignment with proper citations in place, for a lower maximum grade. Check with your academic manager as to whether records are kept of students who have plagiarized before. If so, is your student's trespass a first offence, or a third?

Reflection

What are the effects of student cheating on their careers and society generally?

How would you persuade students that cheating and plagiarism affect their learning negatively?

Did you ever cheat or plagiarize? If so, what drove you to do it?

CHAPTER 12

KEEPING YOUR NEW JOB

■ ■ ■ ■ ■

IF YOU DISCOVER that you like teaching, here are some issues and practices to consider so that your career is not cut short by a mistake.

Boundaries with Students

In the post-#MeToo era, it goes without saying that students are not in your class so that you can date or harass them. But even innocent teachers sometimes get in hot water because they did not preserve the **appearance** of propriety. Do not meet with students in private areas or off campus, except for class field trips. Have meetings with students only where others can see you. If this is not practical in your office, use the cafeteria, library or another common and populated area.

If students show a romantic interest, or ask overly-personal questions, remind them of professional boundaries firmly but politely. If the student persists, inform your supervisor, Chair, or Security.

In Class

The more you use a variety of approaches and strategies in class, and engage students in learning, the less likely it is that students will complain about your teaching style to your supervisor or Chair. Be careful not to show favouritism to any particular student or group of students. Use discussion approaches that encourage all students to speak and be heard, including anonymous device-friendly apps when appropriate. If students get into conflict or complain of being in a dysfunctional group, listen to all of them, and then agree on a way to resolve the problem. Beware of being autocratic about minor issues like when the class takes a break, whether students can use electronic devices in class, or the order the elements of a lesson follow. Ask for student preferences and make adjustments or compromises when possible.

Similarly, rather than waiting until the course ends, ask students to informally and anonymously give you feedback on your teaching by week 4 or 5, so that you can address any problems they mention. This will prevent student resentment growing over an issue that they then complain about to your manager.

Academic Integrity

Make sure you apply your institution's guidelines for ensuring academic integrity. If a student has plagiarized an assignment, document it, and keep the original. You may return a copy with your explanation of why you can't award a grade. If you see cheating during a test or exam, intervene and apply your school's rules. Revisit the chapter on Academic Integrity for strategies for tests, exams and assignments that minimize problems.

Student Success Issues

Sometimes you get a student, or a whole class, who, due to lack of English or math skills, for example, appears unlikely to succeed in the course. To avoid your being blamed for the impending failure(s), address the problem: first, by informing the student by mid-term in writing of their current standing, and what extra help is available to them, and, second, by letting your chair know. Explain the issues, and ask for advice. This reduces the possibility that you will be held responsible for students' poor results, when their lack of skills or preparation caused the issue.

Make sure you have graded and returned more than a few assignments and/or tests before the course is half over, so students know how they are doing. They can then withdraw before the course drop deadline without academic or financial penalty. Also, they cannot accuse you of giving insufficient feedback to determine their likelihood of success.

Grading

When designing assignments, exams and tests, make sure you are clear about what criteria you will apply to student work. Students will complain if you deduct marks for spelling and grammar in an assignment in a discipline other than English, unless you indicated what proportion of marks would be assigned to these issues. Also, make sure that exam or test questions focus on what you have taught. Students should not be asked about something they never had the chance to discuss and review with you.

Grade objectively, giving reasons, and using a rubric or other tool that makes clear what was done well or poorly. Some teachers require students to submit assignments identified only by their student number, so that the teacher is not biased. If a student's work improves markedly, compliment them and ask how they managed it. Substantial improvement can be an indicator of cheating or plagiarism, but it also be a positive sign that the student is considering your past suggestions and acting on them.

If a student argues with a grade, listen and then explain your decision. Accept that you will sometimes err in evaluating and calculating total marks, and thank students for pointing this out when they are correct. Similarly, be clear about your policies for late submission of assignments (they should be stated in the course outline, syllabus, or LMS), and be consistent in application of penalties or refusal to accept a very late assignment.

Be Professional

Always be on time for your classes, with your materials and strategies prepared. Check out instructional media and the classroom ahead of time so that you know everything works, and have back-up for when something fails. End classes on time, too; both your students and the next class and teacher in the room will appreciate this. Don't make jokes that single out specific groups or ideologies. If you write on the board, make sure it is legible, and do not spend long with your back turned to the class. If you use slides, make sure most are interesting to look at, not overfilled with words in small type, or incomprehensible graphs and tables. Put some effort into your speaking voice and presence, so you don't bore students, or fail to speak loudly enough.

Keep your temper with students, colleagues and managers. Think twice before you respond to someone who is upset or demanding, and do not get drawn into arguments. State your position, listen to the other side, and when necessary, agree to disagree. One of the subtler reasons new teachers sometimes don't have contracts renewed is that they become labeled as difficult, not team players. Return assignments and reply to student voicemails and emails within a reasonable time. A typical commitment is to return messages within one business day, and to grade and return evaluations within one to two weeks. Make this explicit in your section outline or online course components.

Finally, take the art of teaching seriously. The first time you teach a course, make notes about how well each class went, and consult them before you teach that class again. Sign up for professional development workshops and show up when you register for them. Ask more experienced colleagues and your Chair or supervisor for advice and suggestions. Survey your students and then work on any problems they identify in your teaching. The next chapter gives more suggestions on how to improve.

CHAPTER 13

IMPROVING YOUR TEACHING

■ ■ ■ ■ ■

NO ONE IS a brilliant teacher from the start. A few are exceptional lecturers from the get-go, but conveying information, even passion, is only half of the job. The other half is learning to read students' reactions, establish what they have learned through formative assessments, build good professional relationships with them, and give helpful feedback. Teaching is a lonely activity: you perform it in a room with your students, and only you and they know exactly what happens. Getting their advice about what works and doesn't is important, but so is getting input from an experienced teacher you invite to observe your teaching.

Learning to teach well is similar to learning to ski or snowboard. The first few times you will fall on your face. Soon, you settle into a groove, following the line of least resistance and minimal competence, until a bump throws you into the air and—back on your face again! Experience will teach you to predict where rough spots come up, and give you ways to overcome them, or at least move with them.

If your institution or one nearby offers a teacher training certificate program, check it out. Ask graduates if it is worthwhile. Just the experience of being in a classroom with other teachers, sharing stories and strategies, is invaluable. If you want to pursue a full-time teaching position, having some certification in education will add greatly to your credentials. It shows you are interested not just in the scholarship of your discipline, but in the art and science of education itself.

Most colleges and universities have a teaching and learning center with specialists who support faculty. Take advantage of them. Ask if one will observe an hour of your class and give you some pointers. Take workshops as they are offered, focusing on the aspects of your skills which you feel are least developed. Fill out the Professional Confidence Wheel at the end of this book, and then seek help and instruction in the areas of least confidence it helped you identify. If learning management systems and apps baffle you, learn and practice your way out of confusion until you can do the tasks you need to.

As well as finding an experienced colleague or specialist to give you some feedback, ask a colleague who is a good teacher whether you might sit in on a class to see what they do. Emphasize that your goal is to learn, not to evaluate or criticize them. When you are watching, don't worry about the content of the lesson. Focus instead on how things get done. How does your colleague start the class? Is there a clear linkage to the previous lesson, and to the next one? How does he/she communicate with students? What adds a little fun to the lesson? How does he/she deal with problematic students—the dominating, the quiet and shy, the distracted? How about time management? How does he/she use instructional media in the class? Or ascertain how much of the lesson students have retained?

Another easy way to get an outside eye on your teaching is to record part of a lesson. You will get the best results with a good-quality camera operated by a helper, but there's nothing wrong with using your smartphone or tablet. The recording will be more useful if it includes some student reactions as well as your own performance. Ask students if they are OK with being recorded during part of a class, explaining your purpose and assuring them that the recording will never be shared publicly. If they are not willing, focus the camera only on you. Give yourself a couple of days until the class is less fresh in your memory. Then, watch the recording, looking for anything helpful to your development as a teacher. Do you exhibit distracting physical or verbal tics? Do you look relaxed and confident? Do students appear to be involved throughout, or are there moments where you seem to be addressing a void? Do you have eye contact with everyone in the room at least every couple of minutes?

The most powerful tool for teacher development is you. Gathering data on how your classes go and what your students think and feel about them is the first step. Instead of moving onto other things as soon as a class is over, take a few minutes to jot some notes as you decompress. What worked? What fell flat? What were the best and worst moments? Are you sure students retained a good proportion of what you and the activities taught them? How do you know? These notes are a form of teaching journal, and become invaluable the next time you teach that course or class.

When working in faculty development, I designed a lesson plan template (see Appendix). The first part is what you'd expect for lesson planning: the name of the course and class, the class length, the number of students, what media or props you will use/need, how you will start the lesson and finish it, the various strategies, media, and activities you plan to include, and their alignment to course outcomes. The second half encourages you to reflect on the lesson taught, including the aspects mentioned above, and issues such as how far students learning went in terms of an educational taxonomy, what got left out and should be included next time, any questions that came up that would be good to include on an exam or test, and what you would change the next time this lesson looms.

This is a handy way to keep track of your various successes and challenges while teaching a course the first time. The next iteration will be easier because you not only have lesson plans ready, you have data on what to keep and what to change.

This cycle of data collection about your teaching and thinking about it is termed reflective practice. It is an essential skill in fields like medicine and social work. The reflective practitioner evaluates the success of his/her choices, and then changes the least effective to see if the new way works better. If you hope to apply for more teaching work, and especially if you want to become a full-time professor, evidence of reflective practice is a good thing to include in your portfolio. An example:

when you realize that an evaluation instrument in a course you teach is not reliable or aligned well with the course's learning outcomes or objectives, you research better assignments or tests and create one. You try it the next time you teach the course, compare its success with that of the previous method, survey students about what they thought, and then draw a conclusion.

When teachers conduct an informal study like this on their own class and students, it is a form of reflective practice called action research. You do not need funding or approval from an ethical review committee to conduct such a small-scale study. However, it makes sense to inform your students of the experiment, with the goal of improving the quality of the course. Any who do not wish to take part can write a version of the old evaluation. This guarantees there is no unfair leverage exerted on them.

2

THEORY AND BACKGROUND

CHAPTER 14

ADVICE FROM
THE EXPERIENCED

■ ■ ■ ■ ■

I ASKED FRIENDS and colleagues who have taught for a while in higher education to share their advice for brand-new teachers. Some have retired; others are still active in education.

I did my Bachelor's [degree] in adult education and I've been teaching adults for 16 years, and in my experience, one of the biggest mistakes that new teachers make is that they misinterpret silence as the students' lack of engagement, shyness, or not understanding. When teachers/instructors ask questions, sometimes they try to fill in the silence by rephrasing the question three times. Give the students time to think and reflect. Allow them to write responses instead of giving them verbally every time, and share them in pairs and small groups, instead of in front of the whole class. And WHATEVER you do, don't go around, student by student, asking each person to say something about themselves and why they have taken this class. It's boring, and people are so busy thinking about what they're going to say, they don't listen to anyone else. The same thing could be established in an ice-breaking activity or short questionnaire. When planning a class, think about balancing Teacher-Student interaction, student-student interaction, and individual (student) interaction. Also, think about the stages of a lesson and what each is meant to achieve, and how will you know that students "get it"?

—**Lisa Richter**, ESL school, Toronto

The work expands to fill the time available. It's up to you to put limits on the time you spend doing job-related tasks. Do some service work, but get used to saying "no" to Chairs who want you on their committees. Find ways to make your courses reasonable in terms of prep and marking time. And enjoy class time with your students.

—**Kathy Mac**, Fredericton, New Brunswick

Figure out who's in your class. Every class has a personality and it's determined by who's in it. Day One is the opportunity to get acquainted: get a baseline of what they know about the subject, and what their likes and interests are. Take some time with the introduction, welcome them, and make sure they're in the right class. Tell them how to address you—I tell them 'You can call me Kristi or Prof. Harrison.' I really think it's important to learn their names. I use a parlour trick—recall all of their names, especially with a rowdier class. It tells them I'm not just this nice middle-aged lady, but someone who's paying attention. In the next class, I pay special attention to the students whose names I couldn't remember in the first class.

—**Kristi Harrison**, Centennial College, Toronto

Don't wish you had other students in front of you—brighter ones, ones better prepared, ones who are willing to do the work, who can spell, who are more open, etc., etc., etc. These are the students you have; your job is to take them as they are and open them to other possibilities. Also, join the union if you can!

—**Maureen Hynes**, writing teacher, Toronto

Engage students with both the content and each other.

—**John Oughton** (my namesake), West Virginia University

Build rapport between you and students early, but also don't be afraid to set limits. Even at college/university level, students can need reminding about rules for mutual respect. It's good to invite them to create (and reinforce) their own rules for classroom management. Also, I suggest always of making lectures inter-active, and in tutorials, regularly ask students to teach other students theory and application of theory, since peer learning is often more effective.

—**Kate Rogers**, Hong Kong Community College

I could write my own book, but I'll just pass on the advice that was given to me: love them and they'll love you back.

—**Ingrid Philip**, Seneca College, Toronto

Honestly I'd say choose another profession! Not enough jobs, poor pay and few or no benefits. I wouldn't recommend post-secondary to anyone. Still, perhaps they need to ask why they themselves are there. That would be my advice. Why do you really want to do this and what do you hope to achieve?

—**Kath MacLean**, Edmonton/Toronto

Do whatever you want.

—**Stanley Fefferman**, York University, Toronto

Set the tone that you want for the class on the first day. If you get off on the wrong foot, things only get worse! Be organized, have the syllabus and outline ready, stapled and hole-punched. I have a memory device for learning names. I ask the students' names as they come in. Then I use the memory system to remember names. First names only, in my case. Then when they are seated,

I say, "Let's see how many names I can recall." Usually, I recall each person's name; sometimes I ask for a hint, such as the first letter of the name if my memory fails.

Begin and end class on time. There's nothing worse for the next instructor coming in than having to wait outside the door for ten minutes for you to finish. That puts him or her behind.

This seems like an odd point, but make sure you know where all the cords are in a classroom. I've landed on my face more than once by tripping over cords attached to overheads or computers.

Use the podium as a tool for getting the students' attention. Come out from behind the podium for general class discussions or to wander around when students are doing group work. Stand behind the podium when you want to quiet them and focus the discussion.

Don't try to pile too much into any one class. Only focus on two or three concepts in an hour-long class. Think of each class as you would an essay—an introduction, two or three ideas to discuss, complete with your own and student examples, and a conclusion that foreshadows the next class. Further, as to marking, don't procrastinate or try to plow through it all in one go. If you have 50 essays to mark, divide them into five piles of ten per day. Mark four in the morning, three in the afternoon, and three in the evening for five days. Presto! The marking is done!

—**Yvonne Trainer**, University of Lethbridge

Have a well-planned syllabus that includes meaningful discussion and brainwork for each class.

—**Russ Kesler**, University of Central Florida

Be the teacher, not their pal. Don't use first names. Never make a threat you won't carry out. Love them, or at least the spirit within them.

—**Cher Holt-Fortin**, State University of New York at Oswego

Yes, never be pals or a colleague [with students]! It gets easier as you get older. If they send love letters and write you love songs, be honest and tell them nicely but firmly, it just isn't going to happen!
—**Kath MacLean**

Get off your high horse, don't lecture too much, and shift to a paradigm where learning is a collaborative engagement with your students. This doesn't mean you're not steering the horse to some extent or not sharing your expertise, but you're all on it together in something of an adventure. You and the class are building something together.
—**Susan McCaslin**, Douglas College, New Westminster, BC.

I would say that teaching is not something natural, but something that requires you to learn not solely by example, but as a scholarly endeavour. When I started, I thought teaching was just something that you do based on what you have been exposed to. It's only through my experience as a faculty developer that I realized there is a wealth of research and literature on teaching written by education scholars and teachers. It is useful in developing your pedagogy and helping you understand that teaching is a profession like any other, and thus requires continual or lifelong learning. I think if I had realized this when I first started teaching, it would have helped me to explore and take risks and try different and new things that had some basis in educational research and practice.
—**Zabedia Nazim**, Centennial College, Toronto

One piece of advice I would give new teachers is to spend time getting to know your learners. Too often, teachers focus on content —what, when and how much should be covered. While this is certainly important, the focus should really be on the learner—who they are, where they are at, and what works for them. A new teacher might zoom through the content and feel they have done their job, but really, if the student hasn't learned anything, what's the point? The teacher and students should get to know each other as people, thereby building trust and reducing anxiety. Once a teacher determines student learning preferences, aptitudes and struggles, lessons can be tailored, resulting in impactful, long lasting learning.

—**Benjamin Laskar**, Centennial College, Toronto

What does it mean to be a professor? What does it mean to be a *new* professor?

Unlike high school, students have chosen your program/course because they are eager to learn and genuinely excited to be there. Right?

Well, yes and no. As in any group of diverse individuals, learners come with varying levels of motivation, prior knowledge and experience, wants and needs, and openness to change. This means that teaching is inherently as much about process as it is content. By that I mean holding a dual focus on how people learn, participate and engage (process), as well as the substantive knowledge, skills and information required to meet your course's learning outcomes (content). In fact, I suggest that the process may be even more important than the content, given the rapidly changing landscape of professional practice across virtually all disciplines. The proliferation of knowledge in any given field is so vast and accelerating that the skills of curating, critiquing and assessing knowledge, and bridging knowledge to application are the most important capabilities students can master. In other words, students most need to *learn how to learn*.

It is tempting to approach teaching from a content mastery perspective, versus from a "deep learning" perspective. Resist the temptation! By all means, prepare lesson plans, lecture notes and course reading lists. But create a space in the lesson plan for students' own self-discovery, peer-to-peer collaboration, and exploration. Include as many questions as answers in your lecture notes. And approach your students as equal partners in the learning process: you have expertise and scientific knowledge in your field of study, and they are experts in their own lives, including their hopes and dreams for the future.

I start the first class of every course with a question and a promise.

Here's the question: "What are you curious about? You've enrolled in this class on [insert course title]. What would you most like to learn more about?"

This sets up the expectation that each student has a voice in their own learning, and that they are at the centre of the work we will do together. It also reminds students that the course is more than just another grade or credit towards their diploma. They will actually get to learn about things that interest, excite and inspire them!

And here's my promise: "My cornerstone commitment to you is my intention that this class will be among the top tier of classes that you have ever taken. I am committed to supporting your success in an outstanding learning experience—so I am eager to hear your feedback as we go, to help me deliver on this promise to you."

While this may seem a tad grandiose, the promise simply reflects what every student yearns for in their heart: an opportunity for transformation, discovery and inspiration. I signal from the very start that I want only the best for the class, that I genuinely care, and that we are in this journey together. By modeling my own highest standards, I set an implicit example and expectation that they will bring their own "A" game.

In short, I think the most important advice for a new professor is orienting ourselves to supporting students' learning, versus delivering content. That shift changes everything, including ourselves.

—**Marilyn Herie**, Centennial College, Toronto

CHAPTER 15

THEORIES OF EDUCATION

■ ■ ■ ■ ■

THEORIES OF EDUCATION become popular simply because they are easy to adapt to the classroom, and seem to work. Many exist, starting with Classical Greece and classes held in the shade of an olive grove. We still call the questions a teacher asks to draw out a student's thinking and assumptions "Socratic." This chapter will summarize theories influential in contemporary higher education.

First is the progressive education advocated by John Dewey, a brilliant and eclectic philosopher, psychologist and educator who lived from 1859 to 1952. Dewey felt that democracy was the most important principle underlying both education and society. For Dewey, skilled teaching maintains a balance between the student's needs and interests and the knowledge and skills of the teacher. Students who are taught effectively become participative citizens and discerning voters who help society develop.

He argued for more experiential, context-based education. He valued the arts and music as part of any curriculum. His influence continues in the current emphasis on active learning and student-centered strategies, as well as the notion that a good education is not overly specialized, but includes some general education and a variety of approaches and activities that develop thinking and social skills.

The Swiss psychologist Jean Piaget (1896–1980) held that social development—both the individual's, and society's in general—is intertwined with educational development. He studied the stages through which a child progresses, from an egotistic orientation to a social awareness in which the priorities of others influence decision-making. Piaget said children actively test their ideas and response and adapt to reduce friction with others, and to gain more positive responses from them, much in the way that, over time, species adapt to survive better in a given environment.

Piaget noted two essential processes through which a child learns: assimilation and accommodation. In the first, the learner soaks up information like a sponge, exercising curiosity. In accommodation, some experience of conflict—such as noting that another person's strategy works better, or that experience does not support a previously-held idea—inspires the learner to change his/her assumptions or approaches. Piaget's theories had great influence on early childhood education. Their emphasis on the learner's active role—not just a receiver of knowledge, but a builder and negotiator of it—also laid the foundations of the theory of constructivism.

Constructivism emphasizes the role of the learner in actively creating and integrating knowledge. Learners use their existing knowledge and experience to evaluate new information and skills, pursuing what seems most useful and essential. They discard or ignore things they perceive to be irrelevant or untrue. By contrast, when something challenges an assumption or paradigm they rely on, the experience of "cognitive dissonance"—an extreme form of Piaget's accommodation—pushes them to change or abandon a previously-held concept. Constructivism also maintains that learners will end up with different sets of skills and knowledge, because what they retain is influenced by previous education, experience, culture and values. It thus calls attention to the individual's learning, rather than overall course objectives or outcomes.

Another influential theorist is the Russian psychologist Lev Vygotsky (1896–1934). Like Piaget, he studied how children learn and develop. He evolved a theory of learning as social and interactive. His ideas were not well accepted even in the former Soviet Union, and remained little known until the 1980's, when Western educators began to apply them.

Three of Vygotsky's ideas continue to be explored:

1. The Zone of Proximal Development (ZPD). As a student encounters new learning experiences, he/she has a range of possible reactions. If the material or skills are too difficult, the learner is likely to give up. If they are too easy, little different from what the learner already knows, boredom and lack of effort result. Somewhere in the middle of these extremes is the ZPD, where there is enough challenge to engage the student, but not so much that frustration ensues. One characteristic of a skilled teacher, then, is discerning the ZPD for a student or students when designing activities and assignments.

2. Scaffolding. The metaphor compares a student's existing knowledge and skill base to the temporary construction that allows workers to construct every part of a building. If the scaffolding is not high enough, the ZPD will be too large, and the student will fail to learn. Teachers sometimes launch new material believing that students possess the necessary scaffolding to assimilate it, but discover that some backfilling (to continue the construction comparison) is necessary. Either the students were never taught the basics, or they have forgotten them. It makes sense, therefore, to start a new module with a quick check of what students already know related to it. This allows a review or lesson in the missing material before launching into the new topic.

3. Vygotsky pointed to the role of the More Knowledgeable Other (MKO), an idea very relevant to adult learning. By comparing their approaches with those of someone further ahead, students can adjust and improve their understanding

through social learning and interaction. The MKO is often the teacher, tutor or another student. It may also be a book, computer program or database, reference material, or the Internet. Many people now learn skills and procedures by watching instructional videos on YouTube, Vimeo and the like, or looking up step-by-step help. Thus, strategies which facilitate negotiation and co-construction of learning, with work in pairs, triads or small groups, as well as whole-class discussion, recall Vygotsky's MKO.

The most influential psychologist of the 20th century for higher education may be B.F. Skinner (1904–1990), the originator of behaviourism. Skinner was interested not in the cognitive and emotional processes underlying learning, but in what could be recorded by an eternal observer, discounting the notion of free will. He maintained that we are conditioned by environmental stimuli, and our actions or choices largely reflect past experience.

His classical conditioning theory held that an organism's behaviour can be moulded by negative reinforcement (pain, criticism, being ignored) or by positive reinforcement (praise, food, prizes, or other rewards). The application to education seems obvious: teachers should give positive reinforcement to correct student answers and behaviours, and negative reinforcement to wrong ones. This works well with simple tasks like pressing a lever or responding to light or sound, but perhaps not with more complicated behaviours such as learning to analyze, evaluate or create something.

Skinner did recognize that not all human behaviours are simplistic, yes-no responses. He thought some learning experiences could be described as chains of individual behaviours, but others were too complex to be broken into discrete choices. Skinner's theories are now less followed by educators, but still apply in specific types of training. These focus on behaviours affecting safety where there is no time for discussion or construction of new strategies, but rather a single strategy that must be implemented almost by reflex. What do you when your clothes catch fire? Stop, drop and roll. This approach applies to training of police officers and military personnel, emergency assistance providers, and student drivers. When there is only one correct response to a given question or situation, behaviouralism applies—reward the chosen answer; ignore or criticize the others.

About as far as one can go on the continuum of educational theory from Skinner is the Brazilian teacher and writer Paulo Freire. In his classic work The Pedagogy of the Oppressed (1968, 1970—English version), Freire connects his experiences teaching poor Brazilian farmers and fishermen to learn to read and write to a Marxist framework of class struggle and empowering those at the bottom of a society. Before you are tempted to dismiss any book that insists teaching is a political act and that learning can free the oppressed, consider this: Freire's book has sold close to a million copies worldwide, and is still on reading lists for many university courses in education and social theory. It has the distinction of having been banned by oppressive governments such as South Africa's apartheid regimes, and is still heavily criticized by the current extreme right-wing leader of Brazil, Bolsonaro, It is one of the foundations of the critical pedagogy movement, which asserts that teachers need to develop both their own and their students' ability to use learning as a tool to identify abuses and oppression within institututions and political systems.

Freire wrote that "to speak the true word is to transform the world," and showed how teaching the oppressed literacy skills allowed them to have more influence on government policy-makers, and on the markets they sold to. He argued that the traditional, teacher-centered approach to learning was a dehumanizing banking model making students empty vessels, whose sole purpose is to be filled up with the teacher's knowledge deposits. Freire's theories connect well with other theories in this chapter such as constructivism, and also with Dewey's linking of education to political power: teaching can make people into critically-aware citizens, who think before voting.

Reflection

Of the various theories described here, which do you find the most useful? Why?
How could you apply this theory to your classes?

Are there other educational theories important to you as a teacher?

If so, what are they?

CHAPTER 16

LEARNING

■ ■ ■ ■ ■

IT'S IMPORTANT TO explore the slippery term 'learning'. A common-sense definition is "the acquisition and retention of new knowledge, skills and attitudes." Until recently, educators didn't have much more to go on. We knew that people vary in the ease with which they can learn specific things (broadly called "intelligence"), and in the way that they prefer to learn ("learning style"). We knew that review, practice and application of new knowledge, skills and attitudes help learners retain them. While we could record the facial expressions, body language, and verbal responses of people learning, we had little idea what was happening inside their brains until recently. The application of magnetic resonance imaging (MRI) and other technologies helped to change that.

We know now that learning is a physical process. At birth, our brain is packed with around 100 billion neurons, or nerve cells. As we learn, neurons extend tree-like structures called dendrites. Each dendrite has thousands of potential connections with others. Dendrites next to each other communicate across a tiny gap, a synapse. As dendrites in a network specific to a subject or skill develop and are reused, they become coated with myelin, a fatty lining that protects them, and their processing speed increases.

So, on a physical level, we are helping students grow and connect more dendrites, and then exercise those new networks until they persist.

Review, practice and application are important because they reinforce the building process.

MRI research has also defeated the left-right brain theory. Our brains are divided into side-by-side hemispheres, connected by a bridge called the corpus callosum. The argument that each hemisphere supported different functions, the left in most people being logical and detail-oriented, the right more emotional, intuitive and holistic, appears a misinterpretation of research. Areas on both sides of the brain are active in most mental tasks, rational or creative. People who insist they are left or right-brained are describing metaphorically how they perceive themselves.

Psychologists who study human memory divide it into three categories: working, short-term, and long term. Working memory is like the buffer in a computer that allows you to store text or data and then recall it, as in a cut-and-paste edit. Performing a mathematical calculation in your head uses working memory to store subtotals, which are forgotten as soon as you have the answer you seek. So does remembering a phone number long enough to dial it. Working memory overlaps somewhat in many definitions with short-term memory, your ability to recall something from within a few seconds to a few minutes later. Nelson Cowan writes that, "Long- and short-term memory could differ in two fundamental ways, with only short-term memory demonstrating (1) temporal decay and (2) chunk capacity limits". Some researchers argue that a healthy adult brain can hold up to seven items in short-term memory at a time. Short-term memory, to continue the computer analogy, is like computer's ability to hold a draft document that you are working on. Unless it is saved as a file, it will not be accessible once the session is over.

Similarly, unless you are given the chance to revisit the items in short-term memory, or apply them in some way, they will not enter the third type of memory. Long-term memory is distinguished by not being limited in capacity. There are some prodigious feats; a Muslim *hafiz* or *hafiza* can recall the entire Qu'ran. It endures as long as the owner is neurologically healthy. So, another way to understand the role of a teacher is this: one who has the skills to introduce new information and skills into students' short-term memory, and then apply techniques like review and application to permanently park the learning in long-term memory.

Another thing it is helpful to know is that our brains are plastic—in the sense of being changeable. With therapy, stroke victims can recover all or some of their lost functions by retraining other brain areas. We also have a better picture of how brains change with age. Adolescents, well known for taking risks, have brains that are still finishing the area related to judgment. The frontal lobes responsible for this function are not fully "wired" to the rest of the brain yet. They have less myelin in their lobes.

Intelligence is not hard-wired from birth. Given a better learning environment or diet, children can show substantial changes in intelligence test scores. Older adults, as the cliché goes, do lose some brain cells over the decades, but remaining neurons and networks compensate by becoming more efficient. In fact, healthy older students are as quick at learning as students decades younger. Life-long learning is what the brain is built for.

Another insight from recent brain research concerns the environment that best supports learning. Generally, our brains prefer lots of stimulation in a lively, rich setting. Music, art, laughter, and movement are the allies of learning, not its enemies. We like to learn with others as well as by ourselves. Also, learners who are tense or fearful do not retain new material as well as those who feel relaxed and safe. This means teachers need to create a safe environment that is intellectually challenging, but accepting of its learners as emotional beings. Teachers who are hostile or judgmental will therefore not facilitate student learning as well as those with a more approachable style.

Learning Styles

There are various theories and models of learning styles, with questionnaires to help you decide which one(s) you best match. One of the earliest is the Visual-Auditory-Kinesthetic system, which assumes that people's learning styles emphasize seeing, hearing / talking, or hands-on / moving. Another model widely used in organizations is Kolb's Learning Dimensions, which defines four phases: Concrete Experience, Reflective Observation, Abstract Conceptualization, and Active Experimentation, and argues that individuals vary in where they prefer to start learning. These are two of the most commonly used learning style systems.

If you show a strong preference for a specific learning style or phase, wouldn't it make sense that you would learn best if taught that way? Visual learners should therefore be given lots of pictures and videos. However, researchers have been unable to verify this. Visual learners given a highly visual approach did not score better on tests of retention than those given a mix of all three styles.

Multiple Intelligences

Traditional IQ tests attempt to measure the aptitude for learning and thinking by focusing on logical, mathematical and linguistic skills. But an educational psychologist at Harvard, Howard Gardner, questioned this approach in the early 1980's. He noted that it ignored many of the other ways in which people show ability, asserting that the important issue was not "How smart are you?" but "How are you smart?" Gardner suggested that there were at least seven (later revised to eight) intelligences worth considering:

1.   musical-rhythmic,
2.   visual-spatial,
3.   verbal-linguistic,
4.   logical-mathematical,
5.   bodily-kinaesthetic,
6.   interpersonal,
7.   intrapersonal, and
8.   naturalistic.

Some years later, he agreed that existential intelligence (religious, spiritual and philosophical thought) should be added to the list. The balance of these intelligences varies in learners, but we are all capable of learning through each of them.

Gardner's theories have been widely accepted, especially in the primary grades, with teachers experimenting with ways to appeal to multiple intelligences in a single strategy or module. This is worth trying in higher education as well. Beginning classes (especially those at low-energy times) with a brief sample of music can wake up and energize students. Incorporating physical movement can have the same effect, especially during long classes. Students can be given puzzles or problems where they have to physically manipulate shapes and objects. It is easy to find online resources with activities and assessments drawing on different multiple intelligences.

May You Live in Interesting Times.

This is reputed to be a wry Chinese curse. We certainly live in interesting times as far as the nature of knowledge and learning are concerned. If someone from 1970 time-travelled to the present, he/she/they would be astonished at how we can not only communicate via text, audio or video from almost anywhere, but we can quickly call up videos, songs, maps with directions, and information about almost anything.

Until the Internet reached maturity and networked devices proliferated, knowledge was a fairly stable commodity. It grew with new discoveries in science, technology and theories, but you stored and retrieved it in books and articles. These were available in bookstores and libraries, and those who curated and loaned or sold you the products were the high priests and priestesses of the cult of information.

Now, we memorize fewer things—including phone numbers—because we can access them in a few seconds from our devices. The Scottish philosopher Andy Clark argues that there is no substantive difference between knowledge internally stored (memory) and eternally stored (in a notebook, device or the Internet itself). The fact that the latter are physically outside our heads does not change their status as forms of memory, Clark says. "And what about socially-extended cognition? Could my mental states be partly constituted by the states of other thinkers? We see no reason why not, in principle", Clark and his collaborator David Chalmers add.

We see this shift in the younger generations. They use their devices to research, to crowd-source funds, to troubleshoot problems, to flirt, plan meetings and pop-up or flash events, to promote themselves, to find jobs and reach out to like-minded others. Those devices, and the invisible cloud of good, bad, and fake information they access, are part of today's hive mind.

So, if you tell them they cannot ever use their devices during a course, it may be like a teacher in the past ordering students to use only one hemisphere of their brains.

Active Learning

Active learning is when students are engaged in their learning. They are making it happen. Sitting in a lecture should not be their only role for an entire lesson, as it does not address much of what we know about how people learn. Insights from brain research that our brains build networks to accommodate new learning, and that new information sticks better when used in multiple ways, support the theory of constructivism: students build knowledge. The result is an emphasis in education on active learning.

For example, take the traditional activity in which a student reads an assigned text for a course. The students who tend to retain it the least are those who simply skim and scan the material. They have done the reading but not added any effort to the process. The active reader, by contrast, uses techniques like note-taking, highlighting, and Post-Its for questions and key passages. He or she reads the introduction and then the rest of the text, keeping in mind which topic mentioned earlier is being addressed. Answering questions or doing other review activities suggested by the text's author or by the teacher also fits with active learning. Applying the theories or models from the chapter to a problem or real-life need is even better.

Active learning is addressed further in the chapter Teaching Strategies. It can be individual, collaborative, hands-on, problem-based, inquiry-based, experiential... as long as the student is talking about the material, synthesizing or summarizing it, applying to a case study, or debating or questioning it, active learning is taking place.

Student Success

Your job as a professor is to help students grow and succeed academically. Students make this task complex because they vary not only in specific kinds of intelligence and learning style, but in other key ways. You can learn to recognize these, and refer students to specialists for the help they need, or work with the students one-on-one.

Some students struggle to integrate the material taught and get assignments in on time. This may be due to stresses in their lives outside academia—lack of money, difficult commutes, mental or emotional challenges, family or relationship issues. Discuss this as a general issue during the first class. Talking to them will help you decide if they need referral to a counselor or financial assistance officer. It may also be that they have never mastered the basic skills necessary to academic success: writing clearly, reading effectively to retain main points, taking notes, managing time, and applying strategies for success on tests, exams and assignments. If this is the case, they could work with a learning strategist, academic writing specialist, or peer tutor.

Another option is to agree on a learning contract. This is drawn up between you and the student. The students agrees to behaviours such as getting future assignments in on time, coming to all classes, meeting with you every other week to discuss his/her progress, and getting some of the help mentioned above. Your role is to guarantee a minimum grade, should they meet all these conditions and the assignments and tests earn the grade. The contract helps the student take your advice seriously and make a real effort to change.

Motivation and Persistence

As well as these academic skills and the necessary cognitive skills, there are two affective qualities that help students succeed: motivation and "grit." Motivation is probably the better-known of these two. It is the gateway to learning. An unmotivated student will not work hard and may not succeed at all. Psychologists suggest that there are two kinds of motivation: intrinsic and extrinsic. Extrinsic motivators are the kind that Skinner, the father of behaviourism, had in mind—grades, awards, scholarships, graduation, and praise. These can be enough to motivate many students to do well. To understand the role of motivation in your own learning, imagine this: I ask you to remember ten random numbers that I read out. You'll probably recall at least a few of them, but after five or ten minutes, they're gone. You haven't *done* anything with them to move them into long-term memory. Now suppose I offer you $1,000— if you can repeat the numbers later without writing them down or using any other external storage. You will probably repeat the numbers in your head until they become a chant. You might make up a mnemonic story, such as "Six brothers visit 43 countries with the hope of finding 15 wise people who..." Now that money is almost in your hand. Can you use similar techniques to help your students retain formulas or facts?

Students have been conditioned to focus on grades as the arbiter of their progress. However, it is possible to add other extrinsic motivating factors. When a student does a particularly good assignment, you might share with the class—with the student's permission—what they did so well. Recognize the value of their contributions to classroom or online discussions, either with a private compliment or by letting the class know. Make sure you comment on a variety of achievements. A student who works very hard could be recognized for consistent effort and asked how he/she manages to do it.

Intrinsic motivators turn students into lifelong learners. These include curiosity, excitement, anticipation, and the love of learning. If you share this love, what activated your intrinsic motivation? Was it a gifted teacher, an inspiring course, a parent or friend who shared that love with you? Model life-long learning by revealing what you do as a professor to keep up. Then, ask students what they love to learn, and how they use this love, or how it affects their lives. You can add things to your course that will foster intrinsic motivation. Think about something that students will look forward to each class—perhaps a game, contest, or some other activity that students can have fun with.

I once taught unwilling students a remedial English course. Its goals included developing their vocabularies and using a dictionary, as their reading was limited by lack of acquaintance with college-level words. I stumbled upon the idea of a game based on my own vocabulary. I set a weekly contest with a prize: the first student who could find a word in the dictionary that I didn't know earned a free coffee or juice. At first, they picked words that seemed hard to them, but that I knew. After a couple of weeks, though, they began to spot my weakness· technical words from fields like engineering, science and architecture. I began to lose a couple of dollars a week on prizes, but I was pleased to see them leafing through their dictionaries, considering and rejecting possibilities. The prize made it an extrinsic motivator, but those students began to see the fun in finding strange new words.

Educators have long recognized the key role of motivation in student learning. Another quality that has more recently been researched is "grit". This embraces perseverance, resilience, and staying focused on a long-term goal. Researchers who looked at highly successful and influential people found that possession of this characteristic played a strong role in their progress. The inventor Thomas Edison once said that, "Genius is 1% inspiration and 99% perspiration." Certainly, he meant hard work counts, but I think he would have agreed that persevering—when the first attempt fails—is just as important. Grit does not necessarily correlate with intelligence, another determiner of success.

You can't instil grit in a student. What you can do is discuss how failure and risk taking are essential in learning. Nobody learning something new and difficult gets it right away. The question is not then whether students will fail, but how they will keep striving after a failure. You might give examples from your own career of when you failed magnificently at something, and then learned to succeed. It's easy to find stories from those famous for excellence in sports, business or the arts of how they learned from mistakes and overcame discouragement. Remember the theory in Malcolm Gladwell's widely-discussed book *Outliers* that mastery of an art or sport requires about 10,000 hours and presumably, many mistakes? Also, recognize students who display grit. They may not get the top grades, but they are in it for the long haul and don't give up.

Universal Design for Learning

You've perhaps heard the simile, "it's like dancing about architecture." Here is an example of how learning can be like architecture. Universal Design for Learning (UDL) is an approach to curriculum and learning media and materials that emphasizes making them accessible to many different kinds of students. Rose & Meyer, the creators of UDL, wrote: "It seemed ironic to us that legislators and architects were working very hard to ensure that educational buildings were universally accessible, but no such movement pursued universal accessibility for the methods and materials used inside the buildings—the curriculum. From our work with individual teachers and learners, we realized that the concept of universal design could be applied to curriculum materials and approaches." As well as better accommodating the needs of students with disabilities (including learning ones), which is a worthy goal in itself, the application of UDL actually improves the learning experience for most students.

A frequently-cited example of this spin-off effect is the simple improvement of replacing part of a curb where people cross a street or enter a building's property with a ramp. The initial goal was to improve accessibility for people in wheelchairs. However, it soon became apparent that others benefited—people with leg issues, those using canes, crutches, walkers or other mobility devices like scooters, parents pushing strollers, and professors wheeling cases of assignments and files, It was, in short an improvement in accessibility for many people.

Another analogy to the effects of implementing UDL is to think of recent improvements to public transit buses. The corridors between seats have been widened, special docking stations for wheelchairs added, and seats near the doors designated for the elderly or disabled. Some buses have suspension that allows the front to kneel, and then a built-in ramp flips down. Rather than having to stand while extracting change or tickets, users can simply swipe an electronic card and then sit down. Each stop is announced by an automatic system, benefiting those with visual challenges, reinforced by an electronic sign naming the stop. The able-bodied who ride bicycles can now "park" their wheels on racks over the bus's front fender. Such changes have another valuable side effect; they reduce the stigma of accommodations for those with disabilities, because everyone benefits from the improvements to accessibility.

By now, you are thinking: enough with the comparisons! What does this look like in the classroom? Why would I want to emulate what bus and building designers have done? The website www.understood.org has a good explanation: "Universal Design for Learning (UDL) is a way of thinking about teaching and learning that helps give all students an equal opportunity to succeed. This approach offers flexibility in the ways students access material, engage with it, and show what they know."

It can take many forms. Posting lesson outcomes at the start of a class, giving regular and timely feedback on student work, and having flexible learning spaces that facilitate movement through them and allow for group work in "pods" are examples. Slides should be designed for maximum visibility, with large fonts, few words, high contrast, and no coloured or complex backgrounds. Videos can be close-captioned, or students given transcripts. This benefits not only those with visual or hearing challenges, but also others who find it difficult to follow what is said, due to issues with language comprehension, or understanding different accents.

As much as possible, both media and assignments should allow for options. For example, offering a document or slide show and a screen-capture video allows students choice. For a presentation, they can submit video or audio files, or perform live in front of the class. Websites or e-learning elements should include accessibility features, and make best use of them, such as providing written explanations for graphics, offering audio versions of documents, and so on. They should be simple and intuitive to navigate, with multiple ways to find and reach a given feature.

There are many more examples of UDL to explore. As a new teacher, one thing that will make you more UDL-friendly is to visit the center for students with disabilities at your institution. Ask them for suggestions; they might have a tip sheet for teachers. They may show you the specialized equipment that facilitates test-taking for students with disabilities, and explain what formats work best on them.

Communities of Practice

"Communities of practice are groups of people who share a concern or a passion for something they do and learn how to do it better as they interact regularly."
—**Etienne Wenger**

The importance of communities of practice was noted by Wenger and anthropologist Jean Lave while they were studying learning among tailor apprentices in Africa. Effective learning was more often transmitted horizontally between apprentices than vertically from master to apprentice. Apprentices shared techniques and shortcuts as they learned them. This form of learning obviously overlaps with what Western educators call collaborative and cooperative learning.

You probably already belong to a few communities of practice. One beneficial thing about the Internet is that it has offered opportunities for people with some common interest—be they fans of books, movies, music, video games, gardening, rebuilding old cars, or sharing resources related to a profession. They can also take the form of face-to-face meetings and expeditions: book clubs, hiking groups, choirs, birders, and the like. When I still owned and rode motorcycles, I belonged to a community of practice before I knew the term. It consisted of people who rode and maintained Yamaha XJ-model bikes from the early 1980's—four-cylinder shaft-drive bikes in cruiser and sport forms. The group's resources included a newsgroup where people posted questions and answers; CDs with copies of parts and maintenance manuals, and articles on common repair problems; and group rides and carburetor clinics at which the more experienced mechanics taught their apprentices the art of balancing four carburetors to achieve maximum power.

This concept is significant to new teachers in a couple of ways. The first is that you can encourage communities of practice in your classroom by giving students opportunities to learn together, to teach each other and the rest of the class. Also, there may already be communities of practice in your course, but not evident in the classroom. Students from cultures that encourage communal learning often form study groups so they can learn, practice and discuss material in their own language and on their own schedule. These are generally a positive development, unless they lead to students colluding on cheating on exams and tests or collaborating on projects that are supposed to be done by individuals.

The second way in which communities of practice can help is by your joining one focused on education, teaching, and/or the specific discipline which you will be teaching. These often take the form of wikis, websites, blogs, or discussion lists that email you a digest of each day's activity. They can also be a local group. One community of practice I learned about was started by teachers in the community services area who were dissatisfied with PowerPoint as a teaching support. They shared competing products, then focused on the more flexible Prezi system, and taught each other ways to use it and increase its impact in the classroom. No one told them to do this; it was collaborative, self-directed learning at its best. Perhaps you might suggest that you and other new teachers, at least in your area, get together once a month for lunch to discuss tips and techniques, or to share one useful article, book, program, etc. that they are applying to their own practice. You may find you learn as much that is useful this way as you do from whatever professional development opportunities your institution offers.

You will also find that, as a group, teachers are more generous than most professionals about sharing their hard-won insights with new practitioners. They may do this through Twitter or another social media platform, through a blog or wiki, or by publishing books and articles. Learn from them.

Reflection

Write a brief portrait of yourself as a learner.

How do you learn best, and most easily? What have you worked hardest at, as a learner?

What are your challenges as a learner (e.g. subjects, academic writing, abstract topics?)

Do you teach the way you like to learn? If so, how can you broaden your teaching approaches to include more intelligences/ learners of other types?

What communities of practice do you belong to? What aspects of these might be imported, or adapted, to your classes?

CHAPTER 17

ADULT EDUCATION

■ ■ ■ ■ ■

DO ADULTS LEARN differently from children? Alexander Kapp thought so, and coined the term "andragogy" to distinguish teaching adults from teaching children (pedagogy). In between are teenagers, who have some characteristics of adult learners, but their brains have not completely developed. They tend to be less motivated and more distractible than adult learners.

Consider yourself as an adult learner. In a formal class environment, what makes you feel ready to learn? As a student, what makes you feel appreciated and helped by the teacher?

Malcolm Knowles is the major theorist in adult education. He developed seven principles, and you will likely find some of your learning preferences addressed by these:

- Adults must want to learn
- Adults will learn only what they feel they need to learn
- Adults learn by doing
- Adult learning focuses on problem solving
- Experience affects adult learning
- Adults learn best in an informal situation
- Adults want guidance and consideration as equal partners in the process.

Thinking about learners' values and preferences helps us craft appropriate ways to teach them. Adult learners demand a clear rationale for the course assignments, readings, activities, and class agendas. They know time is valuable, especially their own. They may be impatient with media or activities that seem irrelevant. Teachers who can't give cogent reasons for major elements of a course will quickly lose their respect.

Adult students are often self-directed and more motivated. They like to have their previous learning and life experience acknowledged. They arrive at a class not as blank slates or empty vessels, but with knowledge that can be valuable to others. It makes sense to find ways to elicit and share this knowledge when it is relevant to a class. This helps all students. So does adding a practical example or anecdote to theoretical content; seeking and valuing all students' experience and prior learning; encouraging and fostering effective communication. You will be helping all students—even the less mature ones—become adult learners.

Students of all ages dislike being evaluated. Adults find it stressful, and may react by questioning the scope and importance of an evaluation. They also worry about their academic skills, if they are returning to school after some time away. They may be anxious about their technology skills (apps, software, learning management systems) as well as their academic writing and research abilities.

Teachers will find challenges in a class that includes students in their late 20's or older. Be patient and listen carefully to them. You might introduce a theory and have a mature student respond: "I don't think that would work. My experience is that ..." Understand that this student is not necessarily challenging your expertise and authority. Part of his/her learning means building bridges between what you present, and what he/she already knows. Such a comment can be a valuable moment in the classroom. Draw out the student's reasoning by a series of questions. He or she may recognize that the principle can apply. Or, by analyzing differences in what the student experienced, it may show where the limits of applicability exist for your principle. When won't it work?

Adult learners also appreciate an overview of the course or class. It helps if you make brief but clear linkages between an activity or module and overall outcomes and goals. Because of adults' practical outlook, they also value examples of how course material will connect to their present or future work.

Put an agenda for each class with estimated timings on the board or screen. After you have taught the course once, times will be easier to estimate.

The E-learning Industry website notes that "adult learning theory also suggests that the best learning environments are the ones that are collaborative and utilize a problem-based approach." This is also called "inquiry learning." The collaboration should be not only between students, but between them and you. Mature learners will feel more engaged if they can make some choices about their learning, within guidelines you provide—an option of two different ways to complete an assignment, for example. They like their in-class contributions to be acknowledged. One way in which adult learners are a valuable resource in your class, even a teacher's ally, concerns group work. They urge their group to focus, use time efficiently, and meet commitments to participating and finishing tasks.

Adult learners will keep you on your teaching toes, but in return they bring much to the class. Involve them. Elicit their experience, recognize their life learning, and a challenging student can become a helpful one.

Reflection

How well does this portrait of the adult learner fit you?

How can you address and incorporate the principles of adult learning in your own courses?

CHAPTER 18

CURRICULUM

■ ■ ■ ■ ■

WHEN PROFESSORS DISCUSS curriculum, they generally focus on either a single course or courses in a specific program. With that in mind, many educators have created definitions along the lines of "the intended subjects or material taught to students."

The reality is more complex. Students' learning experiences encompass not only some of the intended facts, models, theories, skills and attitudes, but also the unintended and even the hidden—curriculum of which the teacher is unconscious. But before we enter those troubled currents, let's look at the headwaters of curriculum.

Anyone who pays attention to daily news knows that school curriculum is a battleground. Governments and parents often disagree on what students should learn. Curriculum, at least in publicly funded schools, reflects beliefs about what an adult needs to succeed in life and to be a responsible citizen. Long ago, in the early grades, this was the three Rs—reading, 'riting, and 'rithmetic. But our more complex lives require critical thinking, computer familiarity, media literacy, group and collaboration skills, and a host of other qualities. Governments consult with employers and industries to determine what skills they look for when hiring and promoting employees, and what technologies are now in use, and then adjust guidelines for curriculum to try to meet those needs.

Thus, curriculum developers play catch-up; no sooner do they finish revisions to curriculum than they're told: "By the way, students no longer need to learn cursive handwriting, or Fortran programming." As well as such specific input, they are asked to incorporate generic, vocational or soft skills: effective communication through speaking, reading and writing; working effectively alone and with others; research and evaluation of information; time management.

Curriculum also responds to historical influences. What was taught in a subject a century ago may still be offered, although in a different light. A student of English literature in 1900 would have a reasonable acquaintance with Shakespeare, for example. These long-running curriculum favourites are the subject-specific canon that an educated person is familiar with. This is true more of the humanities than the disciplines called STEM—science, technology, engineering and mathematics— where practices, theories, and approaches change more rapidly.

When professors develop curriculum, as well as meeting the guidelines and requirements from government and external accrediting bodies in professional fields like law, medicine, engineering and accounting, they also have more local influences. Teachers' own experiences shape what they believe students need to know. In Ontario's community colleges, a requirement for most teachers is that they work in a related industry before teaching. They bring experience of workplace demands and realities when helping to decide what the next generation of students should learn. They also rely on volunteer program advisory committees composed of those currently working in the field to fine-tune their offerings. Given all these influences and guidelines, any curriculum design is a compromise, reflecting many different sources.

After all the arguing, fact-finding, and negotiating, curriculum for a given course is neatly laid out in a syllabus or course outline: the summary of what will be studied, texts and other learning materials, the assignments that will measure students' attainment of these, the specific disciplinary knowledge and skills, and the generic/soft skills that will be developed.

Does that mean that every student who passes this course will learn everything listed above? No. Students will miss classes, skip homework and assignments, and be distracted during class. In turn, due to the pressures of time or bad-weather days, teachers may drop (or at least not teach) some of the curriculum. The course outline is the ideal or intended curriculum, which few students will master. Those who pass have been evaluated as having learned "enough" of the intended curriculum. Only the few who attain an A+ will approach knowing it all.

There is the first of the curriculum gaps—one so obvious we often take it for granted.

The second disconnect involves current events that happen beyond the control of the teacher. Imagine you were teaching Astronomy 101 when the news broke that Pluto had been demoted from planet status. Even if you chose to ignore this event, which probably contradicts the textbook, a student might bring it up. In fact, student questions and comments add to the unintended curriculum, which is a good thing. Students also often form study circles and discuss the course outside classroom walls. This also affects the final curriculum students receive.

The third gap between ideal and actual is where the concept of hidden curriculum lurks. The ideal, intended curriculum is on the table, or the learning management system, for all to see. But hidden curriculum is precisely that part of the course that teachers are unable to see, because of their own biases and mental blinkers. Suppose, for example, that a male professor teaches a course in a technical field. Even though he sees an increasing number of female students, he seldom addresses questions to them or considers their concerns. The textbook he chooses and videos he shows portray only male technicians. His hidden curriculum is obvious to others: women don't belong in this profession. Yet he never states this or puts it on a course outline.

Another example of hidden curriculum is one many people take for granted. In the early years of public school, students are trained to wait their turn, to raise their hand to ask a question or get permission to visit the washroom, to line up, to attend to bells and instructions from school staff. Yet these behaviours are seldom explicitly stated on school curriculum documents. This socialization training is not always negative, of course, but the precocious student who asks WHY all these things have to be done may earn punishment rather than a clear answer.

Finally, a teacher might decide that it is more effective to model a lesson than to state it outright. Suppose that one of the listed outcomes of a course is improving a student's professional conduct. Rather than stating the behaviours expected, the professor always arrives early, prepared and appropriately dressed, addresses all students with respect, and keeps commitments made to the class. This is an example of curriculum that **is** intended by the teacher but not made explicit to the students. If a student wonders what professional behavior looks like, an answer can be elicited by asking the right questions about the teacher's own behaviour.

So far, I have discussed the content of curriculum—facts, theories, models, skills, and attitudes built into a course of program. But curriculum is also shaped by forces not specific to a discipline or industry.

One of the largest such influences is the learning taxonomy named Bloom's after the chairman of a committee of American college educators who met over half a century ago. If you're unfamiliar with the term, a taxonomy is a system—often a hierarchy—for classifying knowledge. The Bloom committee's initial purpose was to ease the job of evaluating student achievement by sorting it into types and levels of difficulty or complexity. The committee decided that learning could be classified into three taxonomies:

- cognitive: theories, facts, models, processes, logical and critical thought;
- affective: attitudes, emotional intelligence, values, feelings;
- and psychomotor, an unfortunate term for knowledge and skills that involve physical movement and manipulation— dance, athletics, massage, drawing and painting, construction and maintenance.

Bloom's initial committee completed the first taxonomy, cognitive, which is by far the most used to structure curriculum. In fact, when teachers refer to "Bloom's taxonomy," usually they mean the cognitive. Later committees created psychomotor and affective taxonomies. None of these taxonomies were based on research into thinking and knowledge acquisition patterns, but rather on the committee members' experience of how and what students learn.

For the sake of keeping this brief, I will not discuss in depth the affective or psychomotor taxonomies. However, they are important and easy to find. The teacher who completely ignores the affective domain opens the door to trouble in the classroom; see the chapter on Classroom Management for more about this. The affective plays a part in all learning. If students do not feel safe or interested, they will resist learning, no matter the topic. Everyone has feelings about subjects, assignments, and teachers, so it is wise to elicit these and deal with them as soon as they arise.

The original cognitive taxonomy is:

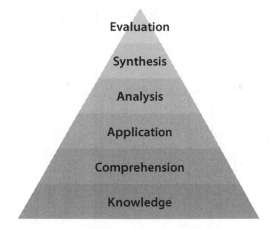

Evaluation

Synthesis

Analysis

Application

Comprehension

Knowledge

The committee's belief was that each step of cognitive learning had to be completed before the next-higher step could be undertaken. The hierarchy starts with low-level learning—knowledge, retaining a fact or statement and repeating it on demand. Comprehension would require explaining, perhaps using different words than those memorized. Application means *doing* something with the new knowledge, such as solving a problem or explaining a phenomenon with its aid. Analysis requires defining parts or steps and appreciating how they interrelate or combine. Synthesis involves combining the new learning with other information or skills, creating something original. Evaluation looks at something in the light of the new knowledge and rates it, compares it, or suggests which aspects might be improved.

Here's an example. Your goal is to teach students how to make subjects and verbs agree in their sentences, so that they will avoid writing sentences like "The criteria is unclear." First, at the lowest level, they memorize definitions of a subject and verb. Next level, they explain the role of a subject and verb and the principle of subject-verb agreement to each other in their own words. Third level, they find and identify subjects and verbs in a series of sentences. At the analysis level, they classify different subjects into singular or plural and identify their subtypes (such as pronouns, phrases, and proper nouns). At the synthesis stage, they write original sentences using all of these different types of subjects and illustrating proper agreement with the verb(s). Finally, they evaluate each other's sentences, for correctness and for how well they illustrate the principles and problems discussed.

Implications for teaching and curriculum are obvious. The teacher should introduce new ideas, models, and processes using this order of complexity, and allow students to practice at each level before moving to the next higher one. On a common-sense level, this seems right. Proceed from the simple to the complex. You can't learn about a new field or subject without knowing some of the terms and concepts special to it. To learn how a car's brake system works, with the goal of maintaining one, you have to first identify the parts of a brake system and list the function of each, and then understand how they interact.

A later committee chaired by David Krathwohl, who was on the original Bloom's team, suggested a revision of the cognitive taxonomy. The members changed the nouns at each level to gerunds (-ing verbs), emphasizing active learning, and reworked the top:

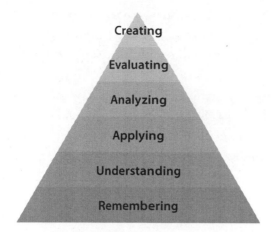

It would be interesting to hold a debate between artists and critics over whether "evaluating" or "creating" really deserves the highest place.

A quick search of internet sources will reveal not only many depictions of these taxonomies, but also tools for curriculum designers such as action verbs, learning activities and evaluations associated with each level of the hierarchies. If the course outline/syllabus you are given includes action verbs for student accomplishments such as "list, describe, compare, analyze, judge, design, explain," there are good odds the curriculum designer used the cognitive taxonomy to develop the document.

If you are teaching in an institution that uses outcomes-based curriculum, another taxonomy may be useful. It is especially helpful if you have to create or modify learning outcomes. Dee Fink's Taxonomy of Significant Learning divides outcomes into six levels:

- Foundational Knowledge—Understanding and remembering information and ideas
- Application—Skills; critical, creative and practical thinking; managing projects.
- Integration—Connecting ideas, people, realms of life
- Human Dimension—Learning about oneself, others
- Caring—Developing new feelings, interests, values.

- Learning How to Learn—Becoming a better student; inquiring about a subject; self-directing learners. (Notice that Fink's taxonomy incorporates cognitive and affective learning).

If you find these taxonomies interesting, and want to see more alternatives, look up I-C-E (Ideas-Connections-Extensions) and Collis and Biggs' SOLO (Structure of Observed Learning Outcomes).

I will conclude by discussing the significance of trends in education. One of the most notable has been the shift from a teacher-centered model in which the professor dispenses the required information and the student takes notes, learns it, and then reproduces it (the transmission, banking, or empty vessel model) to a more facilitative, student-centered approach. The easy-to-recall description of this transition is the teacher moving from "sage on the stage to guide on the side."

When you look at curriculum documents such as course outlines in higher education, you will see essentially two types. The first, and more traditional, is objectives-based. This is what I saw as a university student. There would be a description of the major things we might learn ("a survey of major thinkers and theories in Classical Greek philosophy"). There would be lists of texts and supplementary articles, and of assignments and exams. However, there would be little or no description of what a student might *do* with this knowledge, or how it would aid his/her growth. The assumption was that knowledge of the field was required, and the teacher knew and would supply what was needed. The teacher's objective was that students would learn the material outlined in the description and contained in the required/recommended texts, and that's what the curriculum document reflected.

Many institutions and professors still use this approach. If most of the classes are lecture-based, and most of the evaluations are exams and tests, this is teacher-centered. The recent trend to student-based learning in other institutions, though, has pushed curriculum planning away from emphasis on teacher knowledge, to what the student can do with the knowledge and skills. There is more than an echo here of B.F. Skinner's insistence on observable behavior as opposed to internal states and feelings. This is the essence of outcomes-based education and curriculum. It is has been required for the last couple of decades in the Ontario community college system and is gradually entering universities. Outcomes-based course outlines include a list of the specific *performances* expected of students to reveal their acquired knowledge and skills. A typical course outline might have five to eight learning outcomes specific to the field or discipline. In addition, the outline will list which soft or generic skills the course develops. Of course, you could still lecture about these, but you can't be assured of student levels of performance until you observe them.

The outcomes-based approach to curriculum affects both teaching and evaluation. If the ultimate proof of learning is a student perform-ance, then students must learn the elements of that performance, try them out, and receive feedback. For evaluation, tests and quizzes may evaluate learning at the lower levels of Bloom's cognitive taxonomy, but to gauge how well students can analyze, synthesize or evaluate some-thing, there is no substitute for them doing it in a simulation or real-life situation. Then, they must receive the teacher's comments on how well they did.

When a course is structured this way, the teaching and evaluation are **aligned** with the outcomes; it is clear how each outcome is being taught, practiced, and appropriately evaluated. A course with alignment problems might have clearly-written outcomes, but little evidence of where they are taught. Alternatively, it may be clear that they are being taught, but the evaluation system, consisting of multiple-choice tests and a final exam, does not evaluate students actually performing those outcomes ... so the red light comes on: misalignment!

Here are examples of the different phrasing and focus of object-ives-based and outcome-based curriculum statements:

Objective: Students will learn the elements of a well-organized essay.
Outcome: Students will write a well-organized essay.
Objective: Students will explore the X theory of group dynamics.

> **Outcome**: Students will analyze a group's dynamics by applying the X theory.

Finally, many teachers express their concern that they have to "cover all the curriculum." Often they are faced with courses overstuffed with content, and few hours in which to approach it. There is a solution. Teachers do **not** have to cover all the curriculum by delivering it directly to students or explaining it. Students in higher education can learn some of the simpler material on their own, through reading, using the learning management system, or working outside the class with other students. Teachers should select the most essential and difficult material to teach, and devise ways to make sure students are doing their part by learning the out-of-class material assigned to them.

I have discussed many others' theories in this section. It's time for a theory of my own. Less ambitious than a taxonomy of learning, at least it has a memorable title: The Indigestible Lump. Most courses have at least one. Usually it is material that is highly technical, or abstract, or for which students can't see the relevance. When I taught English courses, the Indigestible Lump often was modules that dealt with punctuation, the rules of grammar, or citing quotations and references correctly. These are not topics that excite the average student. You will recognize such a lump in your course if the students disengage despite your best efforts, as you soldier on valiantly. Soon, like them, you can't wait for the class to end.

There are ways to engage them. Turn part of the lesson into a game or contest, such as a prize for the group that does the best impromptu presentation on usage of a punctuation mark. Break the content into chunks and intersperse them with more palatable or hands-on learning moments. Find funny videos or activities to enliven the content such as the entertaining short video on the reactivity of various elements, *Chemical Party*. Have students research part of the material on their devices instead of your presenting it. Add a hands-on dimension to theoretical material. Also, find real-life examples. With punctuation, it's easy to locate images of signs with mistakes in apostrophes. You might introduce the Indigestible Lump theory, ask students for examples from other courses they've taken, and then discuss this course's Lump.

Inclusiveness

As a society, we have become more aware of not just the obvious ways in which students are different—age, ethnic background, gender, degree of introversion or extroversion, ability—but also subtler ones: culture, sexual preference, gender identity, learning disability, emotional/mental issues, preferred learning style or strongest multiple intelligence. Another less evident form of diversity is students' own educational background and expectations around teaching and learning. Have they been taught to view the teacher as an all-knowing demigod, or a hired servant? Do they believe that anyone with the necessary experience, knowledge and skills can teach and evaluate them? These differences can be a challenge, but they can also be a rich resource in many courses. Letting students speak from their various positions, identities, and experiences makes any class discussion deeper. You have to ensure that your learning environment is a safe space in which people can discuss issues, and reveal something of themselves without feeling judged, insulted or condemned.

Few humans are completely free of biases and prejudices. It's essential that you recognize your own, especially as they manifest while teaching, and use strategies to overcome them. Do you call on a student who is from a minority to speak "on behalf of" his/her people or religion, rather than his/her individual experiences? Do you allow male or white students to interrupt or talk over other students? Do you encourage students whose English is still under construction to contribute to open discussions? Do you address and maintain eye contact with everyone in the room?

Another thing to watch for when you are preparing to teach a course for the first time: are the readings and media materials reflective of the diversity of your students? The longer the course has existed in its current form, the less likely it is that the curriculum designers spent much time finding texts or case studies that use names and images of various cultures, genders, abilities and ages. You don't want your students to experience cognitive dissonance when you tell them that the profession is open to all people, but the course materials contradict this. Keep this in mind when inviting guest speakers, too.

Similarly, examine the images of people in illustrations, slides and videos you plan to use. If they're all white, young to middle-aged and abled, find some alternative images. In technical and scientific fields, the professionals portrayed in class should not all be male. Another point to consider in a course that uses cases or simulations involving families, couples, and parenting: some families have single parents; some have same-sex parents.

To recall the earlier discussion of Universal Design in Learning, be flexible about the formats and media through which students submit assignments. Their strongest intelligence may not be writing or drawing, but they might create a dynamite video or spoken-word piece that meets the requirements.

Reflection

Think for a moment about the best course you ever took. Try to focus on the content of the course, rather than how it was taught or who taught it.

What made it so good? What do you still retain from it?

How can you make the courses you teach more like that benchmark learning experience?

APPENDICES

PROFESSIONAL CONFIDENCE WHEEL

■ ■ ■ ■ ■

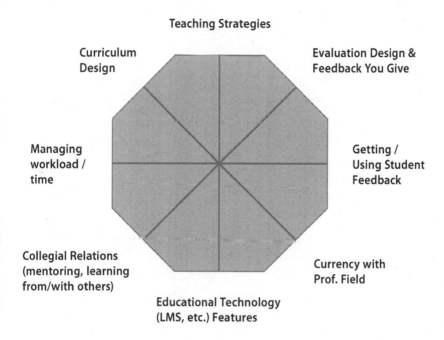

Teaching Strategies

Curriculum Design

Evaluation Design & Feedback You Give

Managing workload / time

Getting / Using Student Feedback

Collegial Relations (mentoring, learning from/with others)

Currency with Prof. Field

Educational Technology (LMS, etc.) Features

Instructions: put a dot on each line to represent how confident you are in this aspect of your practice. The **more** you are confident, the **closer** the dot to the **edge** of the wheel. Join all the dots to see the shape of your own wheel. Now focus on the least-satisfied (farthest from the rim) aspects. How will you develop these?

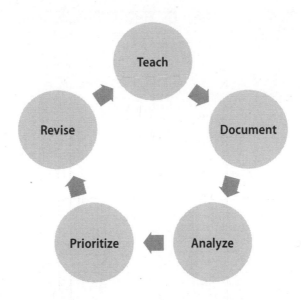

REFLECTIVE PRACTICE CYCLE

1. **Teach:** Deliver a class according to the lesson plan you have prepared.
2. **Document:** this could happen at the same time as Teach, if you make a video of the class or ask a colleague to observe. You could give students a quick survey at the end of the class asking how it went for, and combine results with your own impressions. Or, documentation could take place soon after the class: make notes recalling what happened, when students were engaged, and how well the various strategies and materials worked.
3. **Analyze:** Look at your documentation, and determine the best and worst parts of the class. Brainstorm possible causes of these events.
4. **Prioritize:** Pick one part you want to work on: a different strategy, the order of the modules in the class, a different video, reading or case study.
5. **Revise:** Create a new lesson plan incorporating your revisions. Prepare a documentation instrument for the new part. And, new #1, try it out by teaching it.

STUDENT QUESTIONNAIRE

■■■■■

Use something like this in the first class to gather information about your students as individuals, and as learners. You might add questions particular to your teaching specialty. When I was teaching English, I asked students whether they liked to read (if so, what?) and write (if so, what?). I also added a question about which sources they got their news from.

Your name: _____

Name you would like me to use in class: _____

Your academic program or major: _____

Your career plans: _____

What languages can you speak? _____

How do your rate your overall academic skills? Weak Fair Good Superior

What is your greatest strength as a student? _____

What is your greatest challenge as a student? _____

How do you like to learn (check all that apply): *Through visual media* □
Through listening and discussing □ *Through moving and using my body* □
Other (explain) _____

What is your favourite sport to do? _____

What is your favourite sport to watch? _____

Is there an art (e.g. painting, drawing, photography, dance, music, writing...) that you like to do? _____

What do you do in your spare time? _____

If you answered "work part-time," how many hours a week on average? ___

How long does it take you on average to get from home to the school? ___

How do you feel about taking this course? _____

What can I do to help you succeed in this course? _____

Is there anything else you'd like to tell me about yourself? _____

Thank you.

GLOSSARY OF JARGON

■ ■ ■ ■ ■

Accommodation: creating a level playing field by giving students with disabilities extra time or assistance

Affective: learning that involves emotions, attitudes, values

Assessment (see also Evaluation): ways of determining student's level of knowledge/accomplishment: or, their feelings about a course, teacher, etc.

Asynchronous: not happening at the same time (e.g. an online discussion which users contribute to at various times)

Action Research: practical research conducted by a teacher in the classroom to answer a teaching question or improve a technique

Adaptive Learning: "adjusts the learning experience based on a student's progress. It becomes more difficult if they're progressing well, and slows down if they need further instruction ..." (http://www.educationdive.com/)

Alignment: demonstrable connections between the various parts of a course or program and overall outcomes (for example, if a course learning outcome has an obvious source in a program learning outcome, and that learning outcome is both taught and assessed, the curriculum is in alignment)

Andragogy: teaching adults

Auditory: learning through listening and speaking

Augmented Reality: a digitally-enhanced version of a historic setting where links to videos, audio, etc. are accessed through devices.

Authentic Assessment: evaluation in which students are asked to perform real-world tasks that demonstrate meaningful application of essential knowledge and skills.

Behaviourism: approach to learning that rewards positive behaviour and withholds rewards for, or punishes, negative behaviour

Blended: course that combines in-class and online learning activities/ materials

Brain-based learning: controversial approaches that apply neuro-science to improve student learning

Canon: the works and/or originators who are considered essential or major in a given field

Capstone: a simulation, experiential or other complex learning experience which draws on skills and knowledge previously learned in a course or program

Classroom management: the art of keeping the classroom a civil and supportive space in which all students can be heard, and everyone respected

Closed Question: one that requires a defined answer—yes, no, or a fact

Cognitive: rational, logical thought

Collaborative: learning experience in which peers work together

Community of practice: a self-directed group of peer learners with a specific goal or interest

Connectivism: a learning theory that calls for the integration and interaction of all social and media aspects in a learning environment

Constructivism: theory of learning that suggests we each assemble our own learning, building on previous experiences/knowledge

Creative Commons: websites/archives in which the creators of pictures, videos, etc. waive all or some of their copyright to allow others to use the materials

Cyclical: process of curriculum development in which courses are updated/changed every so often

Curriculum: all the formal and informal learning experiences associated with a course

Differentiated Instruction: "any instructional strategy that recognizes and supports individual differences in learning" (www.learnalberta.ca)

Direct: transmission of knowledge from teacher to student (e.g. lecture)

Discourse: the language, terms, and style of speaking/writing particular to a discipline

Distance Learning: education when the teacher and students are not physically in the same place

Distractor: plausible but incorrect answer in a multiple-choice test

Dynamic: ongoing curriculum development process

EQ (Emotional Quotient or intelligence): measurement of skill at interpreting and managing own and others' emotions

Experiential: learning that immerses the student in a virtual or real environment (field trips, computer simulations, volunteering)

Extrinsic Motivation: grades, praise, certification and other external forms of encouragement

Evaluation: (see also assessment) a technique for determining a student's level of accomplishment

Flipped Classroom: approach in which sharing of course information is largely accomplished through reading and online media—podcasts, videos—and in-class time is devoted to interactive and collaborative exercises, explorations, etc.

Formative: evaluation or feedback that allows the learner to improve the next effort

Gamification: applying the theory and style of interactive game design to learning contexts (for example, designing a review as a game)

Heutagogy: the study of self-determined learning or knowledge

Hierarchy: a top-to-bottom or vice-versa organization

Holistic: a whole-system or overview approach (e.g. holistic grading gives an overall grade and some comments, rather than breaking performances into criteria)

Hybrid Learning: see Blended Learning

Icebreaker: informal way to get members of a class/group to engage in an activity and meet/learn about each other

Indirect Learning: strategy in which students construct their own learning, working in groups, pairs, etc. to research, discuss, analyze, etc.

Individual Learning: done by a student on his/her own (reading course, learning contract, etc.)

Intelligence Quotient: a measure of intelligence that focuses on logical and language skills

Intrinsic Motivation: learners' enjoyment, curiosity or fascination that encourages exploration of a course

Invigilate: to supervise an examination

Kinaesthetic: see Psychomotor Learning

Learning Disability: a challenge with a specific kind of learning such as verbal or visual

Learning Management System: a web-based platform that supports on-line learning, such as Blackboard, Moodle, WebCT or BrightSpace

Learning Outcome: learning from a course expressed in terms of student performance

Learning Style: theory that different individuals have preferred ways of learning such as visual, auditory, or kinaesthetic

Lecture Capture: a straightforward video/audio version of a lecture (see Podcast)

Lesson Plan: a list of strategies and activities for a particular lesson

M-learning: learning materials and activities designed for mobile devices

Mapping: a curriculum verification method of matching outcomes to what is taught and evaluated, to make sure no outcome goes unaddressed

MOOC (Massively Online Open Course): a form of online learning, theoretically open to anyone with web access, that may have thousands of participants in a single course

More Knowledgeable Other: term coined by Vygotsky, representing the person or resource on which a learner relies to make progress—a teacher, fellow student, or even computer program

Multiple intelligences: Howard Gardner's theory that we have several different kinds of intelligence that vary in balance between individuals

Objectives: goals for a particular experience or endeavour. In education, objectives are teacher-based; outcomes are student-based.

Open Educational Resources: "teaching and learning materials that are freely available online for everyone to use, whether you are an instructor, student or self-learner" (OER Commons)

Open Question: one that invites a variety of answers

Paradigm: a view or mental model of something

Pedagogy: how to teach children, or everyone

Podcast: a video or audio recording designed to be accessed on a mobile device

Probe: a question that encourages the learner to clarify or deepen his/her approach

Prompt: a statement, question or case either in class or on an assignment that starts a student thinking/doing

Portfolio: a collection, on paper or electronic, that reveals a learner's accomplishments and includes artefacts such as assignments, reflections, evaluations by others

Problem-based Learning: approach in which students are given a problem to solve or question to answer, and discover their own strategies for doing so

Proctor: to supervise an examination

Psychomotor: the "hands on" or "whole body" domain of learning (playing musical instruments, therapeutic massage, using hand tools, dancing)

Quality Assurance: system for maintaining the quality of academic program through regular program/curriculum reviews, outside audits, eliciting student feedback

Rational: curriculum development process which starts with goals/outcomes, then designs learning activities and assessments, rarely changing afterwards

Rationale: reason for a course, teaching strategy, etc.

Reflective Practice (see also Action Research): reflecting on one's experience as a teacher in order to improve effectiveness

Rhetoric: the figures of speech and writing/speaking techniques to persuade an audience

Rhetorical Question: one that has an obvious answer, or does not require a response

Rubric: a grading tool consisting of a grid with criteria along one axis and levels of achievement along the other

Scaffolding: the skills and knowledge that a learner needs to move onto the next level

Social learning: Learning that involves transactions with others

Socratic Questioning: questions that help learner to clarify what s/he means, or improve an initial answer

Stem: the initial part or set-up of a multiple-choice question

Summative: evaluation that gives a final mark for a course or module, and after which the learner cannot try again

Synchronous: on-line learning activity that is "live", everyone participating at the same time (such as in a virtual classroom or webinar)

Taxonomy: a system for organizing information into categories or a hierarchy, such as Bloom's cognitive taxonomy

Transactional: learning that takes place in the exchanges between teacher, student and other students

Transformative: type of learning in which student undergoes a major change of values, self-perception, etc.

Transmedia: storytelling or curriculum built on the relationship between various texts and/or media

Transmission: direct teacher-to-student learning strategies

Universal Design for Learning: techniques that make learning accessible to all students

Visual: learning through pictures, maps, videos, etc.

Wait Time: how long a teacher pauses after asking a question, before adding a follow-up question, clarifying, etc.

Zone of Proximal Development: appropriate difficulty level of new learning so that the learner is challenged but can succeed at mastering it

LESSON PLAN TEMPLATE

■■■■

Course: _____   Section / Class: _____   Term: _____

# of Students: _____   Week: _____   Room / Location: _____

TIME (min.)	Review (previous class / baseline knowledge)	Reminders of Deadlines etc	Return graded evaluations?	Outcomes / Learning Addressed from Course Outline
Icebreaker				
Learning Activity 1:	Materials / Media:	Student Practice / Appl.	Summary	
Learning Activity 2:	Materials / Media:	Student Practice / Appl.	Summary	
Learning Activity 3:	Materials / Media:	Student Practice / Appl.	Summary	
BREAK				
Learning Activity 4 (etc.):	Materials / Media:	Student Practice / Appl.	Summary	
Review / Summary & Forward Linkage	Materials / Media:			

149

REFLECTION AND FEEDBACK TEMPLATE

■ ■ ■ ■ ■

CHECKLIST DID STUDENTS ...	LEARNING TAXONOMIES	FOLLOW-UP
Know lesson's outcomes? □ Actively engage with new materials? □ Work together on a task? □ Demonstrate competence with new skill/knowledge? □ Receive feedback on their performance? □ Have opportunity to ask questions, clarify content? □ Contribute knowledge, information, opinions? □	Students performed up to level of: **Cognitive:** Knowledge □ Comprehension □ Application □ Analysis □ Synthesis □ Evaluation □ **Affective:** Receiving □ Responding □ Attending □ Valuing □ Internalizing □ **Psychomotor:** Perception □ Set □ Guided Response □ Mechanism □ Complex Overt Response □ Adaptation □ Origination □	Activities left until next class: Review next class: Test Questions suggested by class:

FEEDBACK / REFLECTION

Most successful part(s) of class: _____
_____
_____

Least successful part(s) of class: _____
_____
_____

I need to work on: _____
_____
_____

REFERENCES

■ ■ ■ ■ ■

Anderson, Lorin W., Krathwohl, D.R., Airasian, P.W., Cruikshank, K.A., Mayer, R.E., Pintrich, P.R., Raths, J., Wittrock, M.C. *A Taxonomy for Learning, Teaching, and Assessing: A Revision of Bloom's Taxonomy of Educational Objectives*. Pearson, Allyn & Bacon, 2001.

Anderson, Lorin W. *Classroom Assessment: Enhancing the Quality of Teacher Decision Making*. Lauren Erlbaum, 2003.

Biggs, John and Kevin Collis, *Evaluating the Quality of Learning: The SOLO Taxonomy*. Academic Press, 1982.

Bloom, Benjamin S. (Ed.). Engelhart, M.D., Furst, E.J., Hill, W.H., Krathwohl, D.R. *Taxonomy of Educational Objectives, Handbook I: The Cognitive Domain*. David McKay Co Inc., 1956.

Brookfield, Stephen. *Becoming a Critically Reflective Teacher*. Wiley, 1995.

Clark, Andy. *Supersizing the Mind: Embodiment, Action, and Cognitive Extension*. Oxford University Press, 2008.

Clark, Andy, and David J. Chalmers. (1998). The Extended Mind. *Analysis* 58: 7–19.

Cowan, Nelson. What are the Differences between Long-term, Short-term, and Working Memory? *Progress in Brain Research,* Volume 169, 2008, 323-338.

Cross, Patricia, and Thomas Angelo. *Classroom Assessment Techniques: A Handbook for College Teachers*. John Wiley & Sons, 2005.

Dewey, John. *Experience and Education*. Simon & Schuster, 1938. *Democracy and Education* (1916), *The School and Society* (1900), and *The Child and the Curriculum* (1902).

Fink, Dee. *Creating Significant Learning Experiences in College Classrooms*. Jossey-Bass, 2003.

Freire, Paulo. *Pedagogy of the Oppressed,* 30th Anniversary ed. Continuum, 2006.

Gagne, Robert. *The Conditions of Learning*, Fourth Edition. Holt, Rinehart & Winston, 1985.

Gardner, Howard. *Frames of Mind: The Theory of Multiple Intelligences.* Basic Books, 2011. Also https://howardgardner.com/multiple-intelligences/.

Glickman, Carl. Pretending Not to Know What We Know. *Educational Leadership,* May 1991, p. 4–10.

Hall, Tracey, Anne Meyer and David Rose (eds.). *Universal Design for Learning in the Classroom: Practical Applications.* Guilford Press, 2012.

Knowles, Malcolm. *The Adult Learner: A Neglected Species.* Gulf Publishing, 1990.

Piaget, Jean. *The Language and Thought of the Child* (1926), *The Child's Conception of the World* (1928), *The Moral Judgment of the Child* (1932), *The Origins of Intelligence in Children* (1952), *The Psychology of Intelligence* (1951) and *The Construction of Reality in the Child* (1954).

Shulman, Lee and Suzanne M. Wilson. *The Wisdom Of Practice: Essays On Teaching, Learning And Learning To Teach.* Jossey-Bass, 2004.

Skinner, Burrhus F. *The Technology of Teaching* (1968), *Beyond Freedom and Dignity* (1971), *Schedules of Reinforcement* with C. B. Ferster (1957), *Verbal Behaviour* (1957).

Tuckman, Bruce. "Developmental Sequence in Small Groups," *Psychological Bulletin,* Vol. 63, No. 6, 1965, pp. 384-399.

Weimer, Maryellen, Joan L. Parrett, Mary-Margaret Kerns. *How Am I Teaching?: Forms and Activities for Acquiring Instructional Input.* Magna Publications, 1988.

Wenger, Etienne *Communities of Practice: Learning, Meaning, and Identity.* Cambridge University Press, 1998.

Acknowledgements

■ ■ ■ ■ ■

THANKS, first of all, to the teachers who have inspired me to follow in their footsteps.

I appreciate the contributions of the many present and former teachers who offered answers to my question, "What's the advice you would give to a brand new teacher?" Their contributions formed the chapter "Advice from the Experienced." I also value suggestions I received from Dr. Kath MacLean, Dr. Villia Jofremovas and Dr. Francine Jennings.

About the Author

■ ■ ■ ■ ■

JOHN OUGHTON was born in Guelph, Ontario. He lived in Egypt and Iraq for two years while his father worked on a contract for WHO. After completing a BA and MA in English at York University, John lived in Japan for half a year, and then returned to Canada to work in publishing, journalism and corporate communications. He taught in community colleges for 30 years, gaining a full-time position at Centennial College, where for ten years he worked in faculty development and led new faculty orientation programs until retiring in 2017. He is the author of five books of poetry, a mystery novel, and close to 500 articles, reviews, blogs and interviews. He is also a photographer and guitar player.